China's Maritime
Ambitions and the PLA Navy

China's Maritime
Ambitions and the PLA Navy

by
Sandeep Dewan

(Established 1870)

United Service Institution of India
New Delhi

Vij Books India Pvt Ltd
Ansari Road, Daryaganj, New Delhi

Published   by

Vij Books India Pvt Ltd
(Publishers, Distributors & Importers)
2/19, Ansari Road, Darya Ganj
New Delhi - 110002
Phones: 91-11-43596460
Fax: 91-11-47340674
e-mail : vijbooks@rediffmail.com
web: www.vijbooks.com

Contents

Foreword

This volume and the other works from the research staff of the United Services Institution of India (USI) are intended to explore – from an academic, professional and operational perspective – various dimensions of challenges facing India and their implications to the Indian policy. With several distinguished officers from the armed forces and other streams evincing increasing interest in availing study leave and conducting research at the USI for a stipulated time period, today we have a number of researchers at the USI working on a wide spectrum of topics. Typically, a researcher would go through a structured academic activity ranging from selecting the topic for research, browsing through the collections of the USI, analyzing and presenting the findings to a peer-group and then after incorporating suggestions and critique would again go through the process of peer-review of the manuscript for publication.

Sandeep Dewan's current manuscript had gone through all the above stages with inputs incorporated from many a quarter. The subject matter is also close to his profession – maritime and naval issues. The result of these two – professional background and institutional backup of the USI – is particularly seen in the quality of his work below. With extensive study, copious notes and operational knowledge, the author had reflected on the history of China's maritime power, its metamorphosis due to the external and internal stimuli, blue water ambitions and its implications for regional and global balance of power and on India for the foreseeable future.

Sandeep Dewan is a sailor- scholar, distinguishing himself as a Naval Officer and involving extensively in the research activities of the USI, conducting conferences, writing about significant developments in the maritime domain in the neighbourhood, specifically with focus on China, and in evolving policy options for the larger strategic community in India. Dewan's findings in this work are sober in nature, ie, despite acquiring innumerable modern platforms and enhancing its professional standards in the recent years, China's naval forces are yet to pose severe challenges to India in the Indian Ocean Region. In contrast several scholars, retired naval officers and others have argued that we need to note the emerging capabilities of the PLAN in the future. In the chapter below on "PLAN's Quest for Seas Beyond China's Shores," Dewan argues that despite China's assertiveness, its "current or envisaged near future maritime capabilities do not afford her the ability to operate credible maritime forces to power project in distant waters".

An overall context of the subject is also necessary here. Several scholars had written substantially on various core aspects of China's maritime and naval developments. These include Bruce Swanson, David G Muller, John Wilson Lewis and XueLitai, Bernard D Cole, James C Bussert & Bruce A Elleman, Andrew Erikson, Peter Howarth, You Ji, Li Nan, Thomas M Kane, myself and many others. While each of these authors have reflected on many an important aspect of China's naval forces, Dewan's work intends to bridge many a gap in the current literature on China's navy and maritime issues – with special focus on recent ambitions of China and their effect on balance of power in the region.

At the cost of over generalisation, it could be said that China historically, with the exception of the Ming Dynasty maritime expeditions, had been continentally focused with hardly any attention to the maritime dimensions. During the 19th century, after the two Opium Wars, there had been some efforts as a part of the Wei Yuan's treatises and Hundred Days Reform to strengthen the maritime and naval capabilities. However, these efforts remained short-lived. Despite the Soviet help in raising 157 basic industries – including 41 in the defence sector (and in the naval sphere) – Mao's China considered the ground forces as more significant than the other forces. Minister for National Defence Lin Biao as well tried to usher in regional deterrence strategy in the 1960s but was unable to dent into the predominantly the US-USSR dominated Cold War in the region. The US-led alliances with Japan, South Korea, Taiwan, Australia and others to a large extent constrained the growth of China's Navy. During Deng Xiaoping's tenure, as a result of reform and opening up from 1978, a new lease of life was provided to China's Navy.

This is partly due to the growing maritime trade (as a result of the establishment of the export-processing zones across the coastal regions) and partly to the rise in the sea-faring faction within the armed forces and the Communist Party. The former became the corner stone for the rise of China with maritime trade becoming a significant proportion – more than half – of the gross domestic product and hence became to be factored as a vital national interest of the country to be expanded and protected. The latter – sea-faring faction – is represented by Admiral Liu Huaqing who made long-term projections for the growth of a blue water navy till about 2045. Subsequently, his vision is reflected in modifying the country's naval strategy, reorganization of the naval structure and personnel, hard and soft ware acquisitions, training programmes and naval exercises across the three sea fleets and on the high seas. That the Navy has become of the major foci of China's leadership is also clear from the statements made by Jiang Zemin and Hu Jintao in the recent period, specifically the Qingdao fleet review speech recently. There is also the higher defence outlay that the Navy received recently, when it was termed as a "strategic force" given the power projection nature of the armed service.

A few scenarios could be identified in relation to the emerging maritime and naval ambitions of China. Firstly, given the "coordinated development" between the economy and the military (and hence the navy), we could expect higher defence outlays in the naval sphere so as to transform China's Navy into a blue water capable force in the mid of the 21st century. China's operationalisation of newer surface and subsurface naval platforms in the recent period has such ambitions. This is expected to initially lead to frictions with the dominant navies in the region, including that of the United States Navy, Japan's Self Defence Maritime Forces, Republic of Korea Navy, Republic of China (Taiwan) Navy, Vietnamese Navy, Philippines Navy and others. In the backdrop of the South China Sea Islands dispute, it is also noticeable that the Russian Navy had also become active – with sale of naval equipment (Kilo-class submarines, Su-27 aircraft and others to Southeast Asian countries). Indeed, after the March 2009 incident of China's naval platforms trailing the US Navy vessels, and in the aftermath of Gen. Ma Xiaotian's reported objections to the US-South Korean naval exercises in the Yellow Sea and also China's naval surveillance over the Japanese-

controlled Senkaku Islands, such frictions have multiplied. The Southeast
Asian nations' summit meetings, along with others including China, at Hanoi
and Bali (if not at Phnom Penh) recently proved that the maritime issues
are of highly contentious ones in the recent period. The recently announced
US "rebalancing" in Asia is also in this direction. Dewan's thesis below
predicts that China will, over a period of time, adjust and come to terms with
this scenario.

Secondly, as a part of the increasing US-China understanding on
regional and international security issues as a part of the proposed Group-2
construct, the US control over this region could give way to an augmentation
in China's influence. The reported comments of a Chinese naval officer to
Adm. Thomas Keating in 2009 that China intended to divide Pacific and
Indian Oceans between the US and China is a pointer in this direction. This
scenario results in China making efforts successfully to become a maritime
power of repute in the Pacific and Indian Ocean regions. While this scenario
overlooks the influence of other regional navies such as that of Japan, India
and others, increasing subsidization of the US economy by China and
softening of the US position on many issues is a pointer in this direction.
Dewan appears to doubt the prospects of this scenario in the work below.
Whatever may be the future scenarios, Dewan's work is sure to stimulate
further discussions on China's navy and its ambitions.

- *Srikanth Kondapalli*

Acknowledgement

For the last two decades, China has had the fastest growing economy in the world. More companies are investing in China than in any other developing nation. Job opportunities for people trained in Chinese language and culture is on the rise each year. The People's Liberation Army is modernising like never before. China is definitely a place for people who enjoy a challenge. China is a huge and diverse country with a long history, and throws up many fascinating aspects to explore. It may have been over 700 years since Marco Polo chronicled his travels around China, but even today few Chinese outside of the main cities have ever seen a 'Laowai' because the country and its culture remain inaccessible to the vast majority.

Thus, studying China is both intriguing and difficult at the same time. While echoing the sentiment, Professor Jaeho Hwang, a speaker at the USI National Security Seminar in Nov 2010 had remarked this about the Chinese.... "We do not know who you are...Do you know who you are?" It is in this backdrop that I have attempted to study "China's Maritime Ambitions and the PLA (Navy)". In order to crystal gaze into the future and bring out a prognosis of the PLAN in the mid twenty-first century and its role in global security, I have attempted to study some erstwhile global maritime powers and their rise.

China's Maritime Power dates back thousands of years. China has one of the oldest naval traditions in the world, dating from at least the end of the Warring States period in 221 BC. Nonetheless, China has historically been a continental state with a large ground force and only a coastal navy with limited blue water capability. The rise of modern day China raises considerable regional and security concerns, besides economic and political competition towards finding a rightful place in power politics of the South Asian Region and hence needs a critical analysis. There is also a need to focus future strategies to deal with such challenges, both in the medium and long term. An effort to achieve the same has also been undertaken in this research.

This endeavor of venturing into uncharted and dangerous seas, required great conviction which was strengthened by the people I interacted with on the subject to complete this study.

My sincere gratitude to Commodore Rajeev Sawhney (Retd), who got me into the USI and prodded me into taking up this research project and thereafter kept me indate with the subject. My special thanks to Prof Srikant Kondapalli, my guide and mentor, whose help, guidance, invaluable advice and peer review, helped hone this research work enormously. I am also grateful to Vice Admiral P Kaushiva (Retd), Commodore Sujeet Samaddar (Retd), Captain (Dr) PK Ghosh (Retd), Prof KR Singh and Commander KK Agnihotri who were generous in their comments and ideas while I presented various parts of the research work.

I would also like to thank Lieutenant General PK Singh (Retd), Director, USI and Major General YK Gera (Retd), Consultant Research, USI, New Delhi who motivated and encouraged me throughout the course of my research.

I wish to express my profound thanks to my parents for their constant encouragement, selfless sacrifices as also standing beside me during the ups and downs of my career. I must candidly accept that nothing would have been possible without the sustained support and constant encouragement from my wife, Chitra, and my son, Rahul, who have always prodded me to challenge myself and push the envelope. They have been my inspiration and motivation for continuing to improve my knowledge and move forward in life.

Acronyms

Sr	Short Form	Full Form
1.	A2AD	Anti-Access and Area Denial
2.	AAR	Air to Air Refueller
3.	AAW	Anti-Air Warfare
4.	AESA	Active Electronically Scanned Array
5.	ASAT	Anti-Satellite
6.	ASBM	Anti-Ship Ballistic Missile
7.	ASCM	Anti-Ship Cruise Missile
8.	ASM	Anti-Ship Missile
9.	ASW	Anti-Submarine Warfare
10.	C4ISR	Command Control Communications Computers Intelligence Surveillance and Reconnaissance
11.	CI/CT	Counter Insurgency Counter Terrorist
12.	CMC	Central Military Commission
13.	CNOOC	China National Offshore Oil Corporation
14.	CNP	Comprehensive National Power
15.	COSCO	China Ocean Shipping Company
16.	DD	Doordarshan

17.	DDG	Guided Missile Destroyer
18.	DIA	Defence Intelligence Agency
19.	DoD	Department of Defence
20.	ECFA	Economic Co-operation Framework Agreement
21.	GDP	Gross Domestic Product
22.	GRT	Gross Registered Tonnage
23.	ICBM	Intercontinental Ballistic Missile
24.	IJN	Imperial Japanese Navy
25.	IMF	International Monetary Fund
26.	IOR	Indian Ocean Region
27.	IRBM	Intermediate Range Ballistic Missile
28.	IT	Information Technology
29.	LAC	Line of Actual Control
30.	LNG	Liquefied Natural Gas
31.	LOC	Line of Control
32.	MBT	Main Battle Tank
33.	MMB	Ministry of Machine Building
34.	MOOTW	Military Operations Other Than War
35.	NATO	North Atlantic Treaty Organisation
36.	NCO	Non Commissioned Officer
37.	NFU	No First Use
38.	NPC	Navy Party Committee

39.	OMTE	Outline for Military Training and Evaluation
40.	ONGC	Oil and Natural Gas Commission
41.	OTH	Over The Horizon
42.	PAP	People's Armed Police
43.	PLANAF	People's Liberation Army Navy Air Force
44.	PLA	People's Liberation Army
45.	PLAAF	People's Liberation Army Air Force
46.	PLAN	People's Liberation Army Navy
47.	PRC	People's Republic of China
48.	ROC	Republic of China
49.	QTR	Qinghai Tibet Railway
50.	SAARC	South Asian Association for Regional Cooperation
51.	SAM	Surface to Air Missile
52.	SLBM	Submarine Launched Ballistic Missile
53.	SLOCs	Sea Lines of Communication
54.	SRBM	Short Range Ballistic Missile
55.	SSBN	Nuclear Powered Ballistic Missile Submarine
56.	SSM	Surface to Surface Missile
57.	SSN	Nuclear Powered Attack Submarine
58.	TR	Training Regulations
59.	UAV	Unmanned Aerial Vehicle

60.	UN	United Nations
61.	UNCLOS	United Nations Convention on the Law of the Sea
62.	US	United States
63.	USN	United States Navy
64.	USSR	Union of Soviet Socialist Republics
65.	WMD	Weapon of Mass Destruction

Chapter 1

The History of Chinese Maritime Power

The history of China's Maritime Power dates back thousands of years. China has one of the oldest naval traditions in the world, dating from at least the end of the Warring States period in 221 BC.[1] Nonetheless, China has historically been a continental state with a large ground force and only a coastal navy with limited blue water capability.[2] Although China has always had some interests at stake in its maritime environment, given its long coastline and large coastal population, but history shows that most Chinese governments have chosen to accord those interests a low priority.[3] Consequently, successive governments failed to find significance in the protection of China's maritime interests and did not sufficiently develop their naval resources to protect and promote those interests, nor, indeed, secure China's maritime frontier.[4] The exception to this was the period from the 12th to the 15th century which encompassed the late Song, Yuan and early Ming dynastic periods, when China possessed a large navy, extensive seaborne trade and an expansionist foreign policy.[5] In the first decades of the 15th century, China was the world's pre-eminent sea power. The sea had become China's new "Great Wall", and its defence against powerful land based enemies.[6] By the end of that century, however, the Chinese ocean-going fleet had rotted in port.[7] For the next 400 years, China reverted to continentalism, despite the threat posed by coastal pirates as well as the arrival of the Europeans by sea. By the start of the 19th century, China had lost control of its coastline, a weakness made abundantly clear in the Opium War and the resulting unequal treaty system.[8]

However, little strategic thinking evolved and the navy remained wedded to passive defensive concepts, a state of affairs which contributed to the disastrous Chinese defeat in the Sino-Japanese War of 1894-95.[9] China again moved toward naval development in the first decades of the 20th century, but serious internal unrest impeded modernisation. Beginning in 1937, Japanese forces invaded and occupied China's coastal provinces.[10] Incapability of the Chinese Navy to prevent this large-scale invasion was one of the reasons that it made no impact on the campaigns of World War II.[11]

With the accession of the Chinese Communist Party to power in 1949, the People's Liberation Army Navy (PLAN) was formed around a nucleus of ships and personnel who defected from Republican forces during the final stages of the Civil War.[12] By 1957, the PLAN had emerged as a large coastal force. This was facilitated by extensive Soviet assistance[13], including the transfer of ships and technology, the use of Soviet technical advisors and naval instructors, as well as the adoption of Soviet Naval Doctrine.[14] During the 1950s, the two maritime threats to China were Taiwan and the US Seventh Fleet.[15] Chinese economic and strategic weakness meant that naval power was viewed only in defensive terms.[16] The PLAN therefore developed as a coastal defence force, with its primary mission being to prevent incursions from Taiwan and the United States.[17] In addition, the PLAN acted as a coast guard for the escort of merchant ships and fishing boats through areas where they were subject to seaborne attacks. Finally, the PLAN acted as a seaward extension of the army in the blockade attempts against several of the offshore islands.[18] As such, during this period, the majority of instances where Chinese naval power was threatened or employed occurred in proximity to Taiwan during its initial period of regime consolidation and therefore may be thought to be closely associated with a resumption of the Civil War.[19]

Overall, this represented a limited but coherent maritime strategy that continued in force until the late 1970s. The 1960s and early 1970s was a difficult period for naval development. The Sino-Soviet split, and especially the withdrawal of Soviet naval assistance in 1960[20], had an immediate and devastating effect on naval development and operational readiness.[21] Although naval construction and operations resumed in the early 1960s, the purges of many of the navy's leaders during the Cultural Revolution[22] led to a much more politicised and less professional navy. Moreover, in order to shield the navy from further political turmoil, the Maoist doctrine of "people's war at sea" was applied with new vigour to the naval environment.[23] The effect was to downgrade the importance of training, professionalism and technologically sophisticated naval warfare and fleet tactics.[24] Throughout this period, the technological development of the fleet was slow and costly, and the coastal orientation of the fleet remained unchanged.[25]

All of this began to change during the 1970s. Important domestic concerns included the rapid decline of the coastal fisheries due to poor conservation practices[26] and doubts regarding the long-term productivity of onshore oil fields.[27] Both of these events had the effect of spurring interest in the economic uses of marine areas which China claimed as sovereign national territory. Simultaneously, significant changes occurred on the international stage as well. China formally re-entered the international community with UN membership in 1971[28] and began active participation in international forums such as the Law of the Sea negotiations. In geostrategic terms, the Soviet naval build-up of the 1970s,[29] and especially the increase in the size and operations of the Soviet Pacific Fleet, led to a perceived Soviet "encirclement" of China from the sea.[30] Two key decisions affecting maritime development were made during this period. The first, in 1971, was the decision to expand the Chinese merchant marine and to modernise and enlarge the shipbuilding industry and port facilities.[31] The second, in July 1975, was Mao's approval of a plan to modernise the PLAN.[32] To a considerable extent; therefore, the 1970s was the key decade demarcating a more proactive Chinese interest in maritime issues.[33] Substantive changes to China's domestic political system and leadership priorities since 1978 proved pivotal to maritime developments. Military modernisation has been a stated Chinese priority since 1978, and within this context, naval and air forces have received proportionately larger shares of national defence revenues.[34]

Endntoes

[1] Shaughnessy Edward L. China: Empire and Civilization, Oxford University Press, 2000, p 27.

[2] Nodskov Kim. The Long March to Power. Royal Danish Defence College Publishing House, 2009, p 27. The focus of a continental power lies on the continental landmass. Its concerns centre on developing large land forces capable of securing its borders and establishing and protecting buffers to ensure external security. In contrast, a maritime state has its interests centred on overseas trade, possessions and dependencies. It also typically possesses a strong merchant class, a large merchant marine and a navy capable of controlling surrounding home waters as well as oceanic trade routes.

[3] Levathes Louise. When China Ruled the Seas, Oxford University Press, 1994, p 32.

[4] Mote FW. Imperial China, Harvard University Press, 1999, pp. 719-720.

[5] Levathes. op. cit, p 49.

[6] Ibid, p 42.

[7] Ibid, pp 174-175. There are numerous factors which contributed to the decline of the early Ming Navy. One explanation is that the voyages were stopped by Confucian-trained scholar-officials who opposed trade and foreign contact. A second explanation is the loss of revenue and prestige associated with efforts to quell rebellion in Annam (North Vietnam). In 1420, the Ming Navy was defeated by Annamese rebels at the Red River. This was the first of a series of setbacks which resulted in the evacuation of Tonkin in 1428. A third explanation is the revival of Mongol power in the Northwest, which became the total preoccupation of the Ming court. A final explanation is the reopening of the Grand Canal in 1411 and the disbandment of the grain transportation fleet in 1412, which destroyed the basis of naval mobilisation of ships and trained men. This, combined with the fixation on security in the Northwest, opened the coastline for predation by Japanese based pirates. The response of the Ming court was to remove the population from coastal areas rather than to confront the pirates at sea.

[8] Hsu Immanuel CY. The Rise of Modern China, Oxford University Press, 2000. pp. 192-193.

[9] Ibid, pp. 342-345.

[10] Ibid, pp. 583,587.

[11] Ibid, pp. 599-613.

[12] Ibid, p 623.

[13] Shambaugh David. Modernizing China's Military, University of California Press, 2002, p 226.

[14] Muller David G. China as a Maritime Power. Boulder, Westview Press, 1983. pp. 13-40. This comprised a force of nearly 350 warships, submarines and small combatant craft. While many of these were capable of offshore operations, they were kept close to home. Moreover, there was virtually no auxiliary force to sustain offshore operations.

[15] The PLA Navy: A Modern Navy with Chinese Characteristics, Office of Naval Intelligence Publication, Aug 2009, p. 4.

[16] The Chinese economy was too weak to sustain the investment necessary to develop an ocean-going fleet. Moreover, it was inconceivable that China could have developed sufficient naval power to challenge the US for control of East Asian waters.

[17] Shambaugh. op cit, p. 307.

[18] Muller, op.cit. p.51.

[19] Four events are noteworthy: the amphibious operation to recapture the island of Hainan, 1950; the reoccupation of the Dachen Islands, 1954-55; the Quemoy-Matsu Crisis, 1958, including an attempted naval blockade; and the Taiwan Straits naval incidents, 1964-65.

[20] Shambaugh. op. cit, p 227.

[21] Hsu. op.cit, pp 684-687.

[22] Shambaugh. op. cit, pp. 112-114.

[23] Fisher Jr Richard D. China's Military Modernization, Praeger Security International, 2008, p 69.

[24] Swanson Bruce. Eighth Voyage of the Dragon: A History of China's Quest for Sea power. Annapolis: Naval Institute Press, 1982, pp.206-211, 224-245; Muller, op.cit. pp. 44-56, 111-116.

[25] The PLA Navy. op. cit. p.5.

[26] Yu Huming, Marine Fishery Management in China," Marine Policy, 15, 1, January 1991, pp. 24-27.

[27] Rongxing Guo. Territorial disputes and Sea Bed Petroleum Exploration: Some Options for the East China Sea, The Brookings Institute Press, Sep 2010, p. 9.

[28] Wikipedia. China and the United Nations, available at http://en.wikipedia.org/wiki/China_and_the_United_Nations, accessed on 07 Sep 2010.

[29] Shambaugh. op. cit, p. 193.

[30] Tien Chen Ya. Chinese Military Theory, Mosaic Press, 1992, pp. 272-273.

[31] Dragonette Charles N. The Dragon At Sea-China's Maritime Enterprise, US Naval Institute Proceedings, 107, 5 (May 1981), pp.78-93.

[32] Muller, op.cit., pp.145-155, 179-195.

[33] Tien, op. cit. pp 278-280.

[34] Shambaugh. op. cit, p 192.

Chapter 2
The Metamorphosis of Chinese Maritime Power

The supreme excellence is not to win a hundred victories in a hundred battles. The supreme excellence is to subdue the armies of your enemies without having to fight them.

- Sun Tzu, The Art of War

The Coming of Age of Chinese Maritime Power

It was during the Song Dynasty (960–1279 AD) that the Chinese established a permanent, standing navy in 1132 AD.[1] At its height by the late 12th century there were 20 squadrons of some 52,000 marines, with the Admiral's headquarters based at Dinghai, while the main base remained closer to modern Shanghai in those days.[2] The establishment of the permanent navy during the Song period came out of the need to defend against the Jurchens,[3] who had overrun the Northern half of China, and to escort merchant fleets entering the South East Pacific and Indian Ocean on long trade missions abroad to Asia, Gulf and East Africa. However, the navy was always seen as an adjunct rather than an important military force.[4] By the 15–16th centuries China's canal system and internal economy were sufficiently developed to nullify the need for a Pacific fleet, which was scuttled when conservative Confucianists gained power in the court and began the policy of inward perfection. With the Opium Wars, which shook up the very foundations of the Qing Dynasty, the navy was once again attached greater importance.[5]

The Voyages of Zheng He- The Genesis of Modern PLAN

To understand the modern day PLAN and its operating philosophy, it is important to run through the voyages of Admiral Zheng He and his Fleet operations.[6] As China turns its gaze to nearby seas in search of prosperity and secures its energy supplies, it has embarked on a naval buildup unprecedented in the nation's modern history.[7] Beijing evidently hopes to allay any suspicions aroused by its bid for sea power. In so doing, it hopes to discourage the coastal nations of East, Southeast, and South Asia from banding together or with powerful outsiders such as the United States to balance the growth of Chinese Comprehensive National Power. [8]

Zheng He (1371–1435), was a Hui Chinese mariner, explorer, diplomat and fleet admiral, who commanded voyages to Southeast Asia, South Asia, and East Africa. Between 1405 and 1433, the Ming government sponsored a series of seven naval expeditions. These voyages were designed to establish a Chinese presence, impose imperial control over trade, impress foreign peoples in the Indian Ocean basin and extend the empire's tributary system.[9]

Zheng He was placed as the admiral in control of the huge fleet and armed forces that undertook these expeditions. Wang Jing Hong was appointed his second in command. Zheng He's first voyage consisted of a fleet of 317 ships with a total crew of 28,000. Zheng He's fleets visited Arabia, Brunei, East Africa, India, Malay Archipelago and Siam (modern Thailand), dispensing and receiving goods along the way. Zheng He presented gifts of gold, silver, porcelain and silk; in return, China received such novelties as ostriches, zebras, camels, ivory and giraffes.[10]

Zheng He's expeditions in effect made China the first country to station a naval squadron in the Indian Ocean.[11] His fleet was a technological marvel by the standards of the day. Compasses had been in use since the Song Dynasty. Navigators knew how to determine latitude and maintain a course to a predetermined destination, using charts accurate enough that many of them remained in use in the eighteenth century.[12] And his Baochuan,[13] or treasure ships which were essentially giant seagoing junks, some boasting of as many as nine masts with featured innovations that did not make their way into Western naval architecture until the nineteenth century.[14] If a treasure ship incurred hull damage from battle or heavy weather, for instance, watertight bulkheads limited the spread of flooding, helping the ship resist sinking.[15] If battle loomed, the Baochuan were equipped with incendiary weapons such as the catapult-thrown gunpowder grenades, which the treasure fleet used to shock and awe and defeat pirates near Malacca.[16]

By Zheng He's day, Chinese seafarers plied two established sea lanes: an East Sea Route leading to ports in Java, Borneo, and the Philippines, and a West Sea Route leading to ports in Sumatra and the Malay Peninsula and to the Strait of Malacca.[17] The Dragon Throne's influence permeated coastal Southeast Asia, a fact that is not lost on China's rulers today. The treasure fleet used the latter route to reach the Indian Ocean. On a typical cruise, the fleet would undergo intensive training before wending its way through the Taiwan Strait into the South China Sea. Ports of call generally included Hainan Island; the Xisha (or Paracel) Islands; Champa, in modern-day Vietnam; various islands off the West coast of Borneo; and Sarabaja, in Java. In July, when the winds turned favorable, Zheng He's ships would make their way through the Strait, thence to Calicut on India's Malabar Coast. There the fleet typically broke up into smaller flotillas, sailing for exotic ports such as Aden, Hormuz, Jeddah, and even modern-day Kenya.[18]

At times the threat or use of naval force figured into Zheng He's maritime diplomacy. During its third voyage, for instance, the Ming armada struck hard at pirates.[19] Commanded by the Cantonese pirate Chen Zuyi, who had seized control of the Sumatran city of Palembang, the pirate fleet had preyed on maritime traffic in the Malacca Strait and its approaches for years. During the ensuing battle, Zheng He's warships burnt ten of Chen's ships, captured seven others, and killed five thousand sailors. The pirate chieftain himself was hauled to Nanjing and publicly executed.[20] Zheng He spent a lot of time making the Malacca Strait secure as at that time its importance as a trade port linking Asia and the Indian Ocean was recognised. Zheng He's marines also erected an outpost at Malacca, helping solidify Chinese suzerainty over the Malay Peninsula while assuring free navigation through the vital sea passage.[21]

Apart from its counter-piracy operations, the treasure fleet occasionally used force in support of kings who had shown loyalty to the Dragon Throne.[22] In 1411 Zheng He intervened in an internal war in Ceylon, quelling an insurrection led by the Buddhist chief Alakeswara and asserting Chinese sovereignty over the island.[23] Journalist Frank Viviano marks this as the only significant overseas land battle ever fought by a Chinese imperial army. Military intervention was rare and limited in scope. By and large, Zheng He was able to accomplish his aims through less dramatic means, using shows of force to lend weight to his diplomatic efforts. By the end of Zheng He's tour of duty, the Baochuan had conveyed kings or ambassadors from over thirty foreign states to China on official visits, giving rise to "a far-flung system of allies who acknowledged Ming supremacy in return for diplomatic recognition, military protection, and trading rights."[24]

The Chinese experiment with sea power came to an abrupt end after the treasure fleet's seventh and final voyage.[25] A struggle convulsed the imperial court following the deaths of Zhu Di and his successor, Zhu Zhanji, both proponents of sea power. Ultimately, Confucian teachings which deplored profitmaking won over those who favoured preserving Chinese mastery of the seas.[26] Naval construction slowed down and finally stopped.[27]

Zheng He generally sought to attain his goals through diplomacy, and his large army awed most would-be enemies into submission. It was widely acknowledged that Zheng He "walked like a tiger" and did not shrink from violence when he considered it necessary to impress foreign peoples with China's military might. He ruthlessly suppressed pirates who had long plagued Chinese and Southeast Asian waters. He also waged a land war against the Kingdom of Kotte in Ceylon, and he made displays of military force when local officials threatened his fleet in Arabia and East Africa. From his fourth voyage, he brought envoys from thirty states who travelled to China and paid their respects at the Ming court.[28]

Zheng himself wrote of his travels: "We have traversed more than 100,000 li (50,000 kilometers or 30,000 miles) of immense water spaces and have beheld in the ocean huge waves like mountains rising in the sky, and we have set eyes on barbarian regions far away hidden in a blue transparency of light vapors, while our sails, loftily unfurled like clouds day and night, continued their course as a star, traversing those savage waves as if we were treading a public thoroughfare…"[29]

Zheng He in Today's China Perspective

How China's leadership uses the Ming legacy says much about what it hopes to accomplish at sea in coming years. Economic development drives this quest for sea power. Chinese industry's demand for reliable seaborne shipments of fuel and other commodities has beckoned Beijing's attentions and energies to the waters plied by Zheng He's fleet six centuries ago.[30] Assuring free passage through the sea lines of communication linking the Persian Gulf region and the Horn of Africa with Chinese seaports has become a matter of surpassing importance.[31] Indeed, Chinese leaders have come to believe the survival of communist rule depends on economic development and the comforts it brings to a potentially restive populace.[32]

Beijing, accordingly, has fared Zheng He into a sophisticated diplomatic campaign toward coastal nations adjoining critical sea lanes. This campaign makes use of all implements of national power: routine diplomatic interchange, trade and investment, and in some cases military and naval power. Zheng He adds a cultural and historical element, helping Beijing apply its soft power to the high seas. Several strands run through China's maritime diplomacy. First, Chinese officials and commentators conjure up the treasure fleet to make a geopolitical point, reminding foreign governments and their own countrymen that China boasts a proud tradition as a seafaring power, notwithstanding its reputation as a wholly land-oriented power. It is recorded in history that foreign countries throughout Southeast Asia and the Indian Ocean littoral once paid tribute to Chinese maritime suzerainty through a hierarchical system that was, in great part, the handiwork of the Ming Admiral.

Zheng He also allows China's political leaders to indulge in one-up manship at Western expense, advancing their aim of regional primacy. Chinese often remind the Western World that Zheng He had "sailed abroad earlier than Christopher Columbus."[33] They also habitually contrast the size and technical sophistication of Zheng He's vessels with the relatively backward fleets put to sea in fifteenth-century Europe.[34]

China has always maintained that China's presence and power in maritime Asia far antedate those of Europeans. By conferring legitimacy on interests and activities far beyond China's shores, this kind of rhetoric helps satisfy the Chinese populace's penchant for nationalism, a critical goal for the communist regime now that its ideological appeal is in steep decline.

Second, to support Beijing's claims that it is pursuing a "peaceful rise" to great-power status, Chinese play up the predominantly nonviolent nature of Zheng He's voyages.[35] This helps assuage fears of China's naval construction program and foreign arms purchases, which in short order have produced a leap in combat power.[36] "The essence of Zheng's voyages does not lie in how strong the Chinese Navy once was, but in that China adhered to peaceful diplomacy when it was a big power. Zheng He's seven voyages to the West explain why a peaceful emergence is the inevitable outcome of the development of Chinese history".[37] Chinese officials also intimate that, had the Ming Dynasty not outlawed maritime pursuits after Zheng He's final voyage, Asian history might have taken a different and more humane course under China's beneficent dominance.[38]

Third and closely related, Chinese use Zheng He's expeditions of commerce and discovery to draw a favourable contrast with Western imperialism.[39] Chinese power, they suggest, is self-denying in nature and they suggest that Zheng He "brought silk, tea and the Chinese culture" to foreign people, "but not one inch of land was occupied".[40] They further add that "Zheng He's fleet was large, but his voyages were not for looting resources, but for friendship. In trade with foreign countries, he gave much more than he took, fostering understanding, friendship and trade relations between China's Ming Dynasty and foreign countries in Southeast Asia, West Asia and East Africa."[41] The overt message to countries vary of Beijing's ambitions: despite China's mounting political, economic, and military power, it can be counted on to refrain from territorial conquest or military domination of its neighbours. The implied message: Chinese stewardship over Asian waters is preferable to that of the United States, long the self-appointed guarantour of maritime security in the region.

In short, Beijing has used Zheng He to fashion a maritime diplomacy that bestows legitimacy on China's naval aspirations in East, Southeast, and South Asia, mollifying littoral nations skeptical of Chinese pretensions; undercuts America's claim to naval mastery in the region; and appeases Chinese nationalism, helping the communist regime maintain its rule. This represents an impressive use of soft power.

Endnotes

[1] Mote FW. Imperial China, Harvard University Press, 1999, pp. 208-211.

[2] Ibid, p 233.

[3] Levathes Louise. When China Ruled the Seas, Oxford University Press, 1994, p 125.

[4] The PLA Navy: A Modern Navy with Chinese Characteristics, Office of Naval Intelligence Publication, Aug 2009, pp. 5-6.

[5] Mote. op cit, pp. 646-647.

[6] Levathes. op cit, p 20.

[7] Nodskov Kim. The Long March to Power. Royal Danish Defence College Publishing House, 2009, p 56.

[8] Fisher Jr Richard D. China's Military Modernization, Praeger Security International, 2008, pp. 2-3, 14.

[9] Levathes. op cit, p 21.

[10] Levathes. op cit, p 82.

[11] Swanson Bruce. Eighth Voyage of the Dragon: A History of China's Quest for Sea power. Annapolis: Naval Institute Press, 1982, p. 28.

[12] Mote, op. cit, pp. 613-617.

[13] Levathes. op cit, pp. 19-21.

[14] The dimensions of the Baochuan are a matter of some dispute. Ming histories report that the vessels were 440 feet long and 180 feet wide, a ratio that would make them so broad-beamed as to be "unresponsive even under moderate sea conditions," in the opinion of one modern analyst. Bruce Swanson contends that the treasure ships more likely resembled the large junks used in succeeding centuries, estimating their length at 180 feet. Swanson further contends that ships with these dimensions would have been large enough to accommodate ship's companies of the size reported in the histories. Others, notably Louise Levathes, accept the figure from the histories. Either way, the treasure ships dwarfed the ships sailed by Zheng He's near-contemporaries, Columbus and Vasco da Gama. (Columbus's *Santa Maria* was all of 85 feet long.) Swanson, op. cit, pp. 33-34. Levathes, op. cit, p 19. Mote. op cit, p 614

[15] Swanson, op. cit, pp. 34-36. In contemporary parlance, "compartmentation"—using watertight bulkheads to subdivide the interior of a ship's hull into many small compartments—limits the amount of flooding. Barring major damage to the hull that breaches multiple bulkheads, a compartmented ship stands a good chance of withstanding "progressive flooding" that might sink a ship not so equipped.

[16] Levathes, op. cit, pp. 47, 50-52.

[17] Mote. op. cit, p 615.

[18] Swanson, op. cit, pp. 36-40.

[19] Levathes, op. cit, p. 98.

[20] Levathes, op. cit, pp. 98-99, 102.

[21] Swanson, op. cit, p. 39.

[22] Mote. op. cit, p. 615.

[23] Levathes, op. cit, pp. 114-118.

[24] Mote. loc. cit.

[25] Ibid.

[26] Levathes, op. cit, pp. 34, 144.

[27] Mote. loc. cit.

[28] Ibid.

[29] Levathes, op. cit, p. 17.

[30] Mote. op. cit. pp. 615, 717-719.

[31] Nodskov Kim. Op cit, p 40. More than 80 percent of China's oil imports, accounting for 40 percent of total Chinese oil consumption, passes through the Strait of Malacca, giving rise to what Chinese President Hu Jintao has called China's "Malacca Dilemma."

[32] Ibid. pp 44-45.

[33] Levathes, op. cit, pp. 20-22.

[34] Ibid.

[35] Mote. op. cit. p. 616. The "peaceful rise" hypothesis rests on several assumptions and projections. First, China needs a stable external environment to develop its economy. Second, Beijing faces severe internal problems that will distract it from hegemonic ambitions. Third, China's rise to a "middle rung of advanced nations" will take 15-20 years, by which time the country will be fully integrated into the international system. Finally, China's military growth is proportionate to the vastness of the country in terms of both geography and population. In recent months Beijing, apparently concerned about the misgivings the notion of China's "rise" provokes, have officially recast China's policy as one of "peaceful development." See also Hayoun Jessie Ryou, "The Meaning of China's 'Peaceful Development' Concept, ORF Occasional Paper 12, Nov 2009.

[36] Cole Bernard D. The Great Wall at Sea: China's Navy Enters the Twenty-first Century, Annapolis: Naval Institute Press, 2001, pp. 3, 17.

[37] Mote. op. cit. pp. 616-617.

[38] Levathes, op. cit, p. 20.

[39] Mote. loc. cit.

[40] Ibid.

[41] Ibid.

Chapter 3

The Evolution of the People's Liberation Army Navy

"We must build a strong navy for the purpose of fighting against imperialist aggression."[1]

...........*Mao Zedong*

In consonance with Mao's vision for China post the revolution, the PLAN was established with Soviet assistance obtained by Mao Zedong during his 1949-50 visit to Moscow and he planned to use half of the initial Soviet loan of $ 300 million to purchase naval equipment.[2]

The PLAN Air Force (PLANAF) was added two years later.[3] By 1954 an estimated 2,500 Soviet naval advisers were in China, possibly one adviser to every thirty Chinese naval personnel, and the Soviet Union began providing modern ships.[4] With Soviet assistance, the navy reorganised in 1954 and 1955 into the North Sea Fleet, East Sea Fleet, and South Sea Fleet, and a corps of admirals and other naval officers was established from the ranks of the ground forces.[5]

The Chinese Navy imported equipment and technology from the Soviet Union when it was first established in the 1950s and developed the ability to make naval equipment with Chinese parts in a short time. In shipbuilding the Soviets first assisted the Chinese, then the Chinese copied Soviet designs without assistance, and finally the Chinese produced vessels of their own design.[6]

A procurement policy was drawn up in August 1950 by the PLAN to build a light-duty surface warfare force. Such a force was to consist of air, submarine, and torpedo boat elements. For the construction of new vessels, the Bureau of Shipbuilding Industry was created in October 1950 and was based in Shanghai.[7] With the guidance of the Soviets, the Chinese developed a joint agreement with the Soviet Union for the license production of five different kinds of ships in the Soviet Navy in June 1953 namely frigates, medium submarines, minesweepers, corvettes and torpedo boats.[8]

The Shipbuilding Industry Management Bureau in 1954 created the Ship Product Design Branch, which later was renamed the First Ship Product Design Office. The Bureau built and operated six shipyards and two construction sites for the PLAN. From 1955 to 1960, the shipyards produced more than 100 ships. In 1954, the Ship Model Testing Institute was created by the First Ministry of Machine Building (MMB). The same institute was enlarged and renamed the Ship Science Research Institute of the First MMB and the Ministry of Communication. The MMB organised the Ship Product Design Institute with four additional institutes in 1958.[9]

The PLAN from 1958 onwards developed research institutes dedicated to the study of ship design, underwater weapons, hydro-acoustics, and navigation. The PLAN developed the Science and Technology Research Division. Universities in Shanghai, Xian, Dalian, and Wuhan developed research bodies dedicated to the study of shipbuilding, naval weapon systems, and training equipment. "The Agreement on the Assistance to the People's Republic of China by Union of Soviet Socialist Republics (USSR) for Building Warships by the Chinese Navy" was signed on February 4, 1959 between China and the Soviet Union, which allowed the Chinese to begin receiving designs and parts for the license production of submarines, two kinds of guided missile ships, and a hydro-foil torpedo boat.[10]

The Navy Party Committee (NPC) submitted a report to the Central Military Commission (CMC) to clearly define the policy goals of their naval modernisation, which included: the development of guided missile capabilities, and the continual development of the navy's conventional equipment, the creation of a submarine force, the development of small and medium sized surface ships. The Ship Industrial Management Bureau was absorbed by the Third MMB in 1960, whereas the Military Ship Overall Design Office, which was under the Ship Product Design Institute, was expanded into seven offices with new emphasis on the development of torpedoes and navigational instruments. Additionally, a test base for the development of large ships was created in Wuxi, which helped lay the course for more research and development.[11]

Through the upheavals of the late 1950s and 1960s the Navy remained relatively undisturbed. Under the leadership of Minister of National Defense Lin Biao, large investments were made in naval construction during the frugal years immediately after the Great Leap Forward.[12] During the Cultural Revolution, a number of top naval commissars and commanders were purged, and naval forces were used to suppress a revolt in Wuhan in July 1967, but the service largely avoided the turmoil. Although it paid lip service to Mao and assigned political commissars aboard ships, the Navy continued to train, build, and maintain the fleets.[13] In August 1960, the Soviet Union retracted its support of the Chinese in the development of the PLAN by pulling its advisors and ceasing the supply of technology and materials, forcing China to develop its navy by itself. As a solution, the Chinese created research bodies to fill the gap that Soviet Union had left in research and development in order to continue the modernisation and development of its navy. The Warship Research Academy, or the Seventh Academy of the Ministry of National Defence, was created in June 1961. The Seventh Academy focused on research and development of ships, weapons systems, equipment, and the assimilation of imported technology.[14]

The Seventh Academy was also responsible for the creation of other research institutes dedicated to creating various ship designs, including nuclear submarines and propulsion systems. Additional research institutions were created after 1963, when the Sixth MMB was created. These institutes were specialised in various aspects of naval research, such as machine building, instruments, technology, and information.[15]

The cumulative efforts of the various research bodies helped China become more capable of domestically developing a navy by duplicating imported technology and producing needed parts. By the mid-1960s, the Seventh Academy became capable of developing China's first-generation of naval vessels, such as nuclear power submarines, survey ships, destroyers, frigates, and various naval weapons systems.[16]

In the 1970s, when approximately 20 percent of the defense budget allocated to naval forces, the Navy grew dramatically. The conventional submarine force grew in numbers as did the number of missile-carrying ships. Also the production of larger surface ships, including support ships for oceangoing operations, increased. The Navy also began development of nuclear powered attack submarines (SSN) and nuclear-powered ballistic missile submarines (SSBN). However, the PLAN lacked surface-to-air missile (SAM) protection for its ships, which were equipped solely with guns and had no surface-to-surface missiles (SSMs). It also had very little anti-submarine warfare (ASW) capability.[17]

In the 1980s the Navy was developing into a regional naval power with some green-water capabilities. Naval construction continued at a level somewhat below the 1970s rate. Modernisation efforts encompassed higher educational and technical standards for personnel; reformulation of the traditional coastal defense doctrine and force structure in favour of more blue-water operations; and training in naval combined-arms operations involving submarine, surface, naval aviation, and coastal defense forces. Examples of the expansion of China's blue-water naval capabilities were the 1980 recovery of an intercontinental ballistic missile (ICBM) in the Western Pacific by a twenty-ship fleet, extended naval operations in the South China Sea in 1984 and 1985, and the visit of two naval ships to three South Asian nations in 1985.[18] In 1982 the Navy conducted a successful test of an underwater-launched ballistic missile; in 1986 the Navy's order of battle included at least one Xia-class SSBNs armed with twelve CSS-NX-4 missiles and five Han-class SSNs armed with six SY-2 cruise missiles. The Navy also had some success in developing a variety of ship-to-ship, ship-to-shore, shore-to-ship, and air-to-ship missiles. In the late 1980s, major deficiencies reportedly remained in antisubmarine warfare, mine warfare, naval electronics including electronic countermeasures equipment and naval aviation capabilities.[19]

In April 2010, the PLAN held a fleet review in Qingdao for its 60th anniversary celebrations, displaying some of its latest warships and submarines, such as the Type-052C Luyang II-class Guided Missile Destroyers (DDG), Type-051C Luzhou-class DDG and Type-054A Jiangkai-class frigates. The Chinese surface force is currently estimated by the US Department of Defence to have around 75 major surface combatants. Additionally, there are approximately 45 coastal missile-patrol craft and 50 medium and heavy amphibious-lift vessels, whose numbers have been increasing over recent years. The submarine fleet is also undergoing rapid expansion, with five types of nuclear and conventional submarines under procurement, including the Jin-class SSBN, Shang-class SSN, and improved Song, Yuan and Russian Kilo class submarines. Moreover, growing official public discussion of the acquisition of an aircraft-carrier force appears to be paving the way for a programme go-ahead in the near future. Senior Chinese navy officials have said that the local shipbuilding industry has actively conducted research into aircraft-carrier construction and should be ready to operate the refurbished former Ukrainian aircraft carrier, Varyag, by the middle of this decade.[20]

Modern PLAN's Forces, Operations, Exercises and Training

Naval Forces

The PLAN, which was once a subordinate force to the PLA Ground Force and played a limited role during the Cold-war era, is being transformed into a global naval power. China began modernising its naval forces in the 1990s in an effort to build a Blue Water PLAN that would take up operations beyond its territorial waters.[21] China continues to build the most diverse and apparently powerful naval force in the entire Asian region to stake its claim in the resource rich East and South China Seas. With the intent to secure its strategic oil and energy routes in the Arabian Sea and Indian Ocean, China has built and sought foreign bases in the IOR in recent times.[22]

The modernisation programme, involving acquisition and deployment of an increased number of frigates, destroyers, submarines, aircraft carriers, manned and unmanned aircraft along with a broad range of weapons, especially ballistic and cruise missiles, has projected China as a major naval power in the world.

The PLAN is divided into three fleets the North Sea, East Sea and South China Sea fleets. The North Sea Fleet is headquartered at Qingdao, the East Sea Fleet at Shanghai, and the South Sea Fleet at Guangzhou. The PLAN also has the Marine Force, naval aviation wing and a Coastal Defence force. It has major naval bases at Lushun, Huludao, Qingdao, Shanghai, Zhou Shan, Wenzhou, Xiamen, Guangzhou, Zhanjiang, and Yulin.

The PLAN possesses one (under trial and yet to be operationalised) aircraft carrier, around 79 main surface combatants comprising destroyers and frigates, 5 nuclear powered and 60 conventional submarines, 20 large and 49 medium amphibious landing ships, and 86 missile-equipped patrol craft. The PLAN's aircraft carrier, a renovated Kuznetsov hull, began sea trials in 2011. Once China deploys aircraft capable of operating from a carrier, it would afford PLAN the capability for carrier-based air operations. However, it will take several years for China to achieve a minimal level of combat capability and fleet integration for its aircraft carrier.[23]

The PLAN is improving its long-range surveillance capability with sky-wave and surface wave over-the-horizon (OTH) radars. In combination with early-warning aircraft, unmanned aerial vehicles (UAVs), and other surveillance and reconnaissance equipment, the radars would allow the PLAN to carry out surveillance and reconnaissance over the Western Pacific. These radars can be used in conjunction with reconnaissance satellites to locate targets at great distances from China, thereby supporting long-range precision strikes, including employment of ASBMs.[24]

The modern day PLAN primarily focuses on improving anti-air and anti-surface warfare capabilities, as well as developing a credible at-sea nuclear deterrent. The additional attack submarines, multi-mission surface combatants, and fourth-generation naval aircraft entering the force are designed to achieve sea superiority within the first island chain and counter any potential intervention in the event of a Taiwan conflict. The PLAN is also acquiring ships capable of supporting conventional military operations and HA/DR missions, including several amphibious transport docks and the Anwei-class (Peace Ark) hospital ship.[25]

The PLAN has the following new acquisitions and procurements planned over the next few years. Three guided missile Type 059 class frigates are under construction and are likely to be commissioned by 2015. Two type 052C class destroyers are under construction and are scheduled to be commissioned in early 2013. Plans are on to induct around 60 more Type 022 Houbei fast attack craft. The second of three Type 071 Yuzhao amphibious ships (landing platform dock) has been launched recently. Three Type 095 Jin Class SSBNs are under construction and are likely to be commissioned by 2018. This particular construction programme is reportedly running behind schedule and is facing problems of weaponisation. 15 Yuan-class (Type 041) SSKs are estimated to be constructed and inducted in the coming decade. A new conventional SSK submarine is under construction at the Wuhan Shipyard since September 2010. This is the third SSK design of the series unveiled by China since 1994. Three more Jin Class SSBNs are under construction.[26]

In the aircraft holding, upgraded J-10A and J-10S naval fighters have been recently unveiled. J-11BH and J-11BS fighters were acquired by the PLAN Naval Force (PLANAF) in 2010. The JL-9/JJ-9 trainers were acquired by the PLAN in 2011.[27] The PLAN has last year unveiled the J-15 which is likely to serve her carrier air wing. This is the PLAN developed naval version of the indigenous J-11B aircraft. It is an upgraded version of the Russian SU-33 with a heavier landing gear, tail hook, folding wings, and other characteristics necessary for air operations aboard the carrier, and appears to have Active Electronically Scanned Array (AESA) radar, newer avionics and controls, and potentially more range.[28]

Naval Combatants and Auxiliary Holding			
Category	Name	In Service	On Order
Destroyers	Luzhou Class Type 051C	2	
	Hangzhou Class (Soveremenny)	4	
	Luyang II Class Type 052C	3	2
	Luyang I Class Type 052B	2	
	Luhai Class Type 052A	1	
	Luhu Class Type 052	2	
	Luda Class Type 051	14	
Frigates	Jiangkai Type 054	12	16
	Jiangwei III Class Type 059	-	3
	Jiangwei II Class Type 057	10	
	Jiangwei I Class Type 055	8	
	Jianghu Class Type 053	23	
Patrol Craft	Type 22 Houbei class	60	60
	Houjian Class Type 037-II	7	
	Houxin Class Type 037-IG	16	
	Haiqing Type 037-IS	25	20
	Hainan Type 037	78	
	Shanghai III / Haijui Type 062 / 1	17	
	Shanghai II Type 062	35	
Submarines	SSBN Jin Class	2	3
	SSBN Xia	1	
	SSB Golf	1	
	SSN Shang Type 093	3	

	SSN Han Type 091	4	
	Kilo Class Project EKM 877 & 636	12	
	Song Class Improved	-	5
	SS Yuan Class Type 041	2	
	SS Song Class Type 039	19	
	SS Ming Class Type 035	17	
Amphibious Craft	LPD Yuzhao Type 071	1	2
	LST Yukan/ Yutin	26	
	LSM	28	
Patrol Hydrofoil	Huchun Class	90	
Mine Sweepers/Hunters	Wolei / Bulieijian	1	
	Type 010 [Sov T-43]	40	
	Wosao Class Type 082	4	
	Lianyun Class (minesweeper-coastal)	50	
Auxiliary Ship	Oiler/Cargo	46	
	Survey (Ocean/Hydro) Ship	35	13
	Hospital Ships	4	
	Recognition / surveillance / Intelligence	21	
	Space and Missile Tracking Ship	5	

Naval Aviation Holding

Category	Name	In Service	On Order
Bomber/Anti-ship strike	Su-30 Mk2	24	
	Su-33 (Ship borne)	-	12
	H5	20	
	H6	30	
	JH-7	84	
Fighter/ground Strike fighter	J7	36	
	Q5	30	
	J8 II	48	
Maritime Patrol/ASW			
	SH5	4	
	Y-8 MPA	6	
Helicopter	Z-8 Super Frelon	25	
	Z9	25	
	Ka-27	3	
	Ka-28	13	8
	SA 321	15	
Transport Aircraft	Y5	50	
	Y7	10	
	Y8	4	
	Li2	2	

PLAN Operations, Exercises, Deployments and Maritime Diplomacy

The PLAN has been the most visible arm of the Chinese military on the global stage through its port calls, exercises with international partners, and participation in overseas operations such as the Gulf of Aden anti-piracy mission and civilian evacuation operations off Libya.[31] Of these international engagements, the anti-piracy deployment in particular has led to some impor-tant lessons for the PLAN. The importance of logistics for deployed platforms during extended deployments has been very aptly reinforced. Due to China's long-held stance on not establishing over-seas military bases, the PLAN has had to rely on commercial ports and agreements for its replenishment, such as in Salalah, Oman. Also, the anti-piracy patrol has led to the improvement of the PLAN's emergency medical evacuation and major engineering repair capabilities due to specific events which have occurred during the deployments. Overall, these ongoing deployments have contributed to the PLAN's ability to maintain itself at sea for longer periods of time, develop realistic exercises based on the operation at hand, and have given it the opportunity to interact with other major navies of the world. Broadly, these operations have contributed to the PLAN's better learning of how to operate in distant seas, an area of ever-expanding importance, due to China's increased interests and presence overseas. These operations will continue to carry the PLAN beyond "offshore defense" and into a more global, expeditionary navy.[32]

Towards becoming a more visible navy as also increasing its navy to navy contact, the PLAN's development, complexity, length, and multiunit participation in naval exercises has been continuously increasing. The PLAN's training continues to develop in terms of joint training, military operations other than war (MOOTW), civilian integration in military operations, training according to doctrine, and training under "real-war" conditions. This training has led to improvements in professionalism and the PLAN's ability to perform in all areas of naval warfare. Furthermore, regional naval exercises are increasingly being employed to send political signals to the United States and other countries in the Asia Pacific through an increased PLAN presence in the region.[33]

The PLAN has been learning from its domestic and international exercises as well as its noncombat operations. The increasingly expeditionary nature of the PLAN operations is worth a mention. Whether it be through the PLAN's participation in the overseas anti-piracy mission, the participation in multinational exercises abroad, participation in MOOTW operations, the development of PLAN logistics, or even PLAN trans regional domestic exercises, all of these operations and exercises have significant implications for the PLAN's ability and willingness to project its power and increase its presence beyond China's defended territory. As these efforts appear likely to transition into more "combat-like" operations in the future, given China's expanding interests and presence, outside observers must continue to analyse the PLAN's ability to translate its lessons from these simulations and noncombat situations into effectiveness in actual deployments, especially in terms of how it may overcome its lack of overseas bases when projecting power abroad.[34]

Since the last decade the PLAN has increasingly focused on naval diplomacy and exercises with regional partners and major maritime powers. In 2005, the PLAN joined Russian Navy counterparts in "Peace Mission 2005" conducting firepower demonstrations for the first time with a major foreign navy.[35] The 2010 White Paper on China's Defence states that over the past two years, the PLAN conducted maritime training exercises with 24 countries. Many of these activities are focused on reassuring neighbours of the PLAN's benign intent in the maritime realm, but they also provide an operationally inexperienced navy with much-needed foreign expertise.[36]

It is debatable whether or not expanding Chinese economic interests would necessitate the PLAN to possess capability to conduct sea control and air superiority operations along SLOCs in the Philippine Sea, Straits of Malacca, and the Indian Ocean region. The PLAN would need to strategise regarding military and non-military approaches to the perceived vulnerabilities in these areas. Given national development priorities, it is unlikely that China would pursue the extremely high cost of transition to a carrier navy for at least the next ten to fifteen years.[37] A one/two operational carrier PLAN will lend prestige to China's international standing. It would also afford the PLAN extended airpower in scenarios where China can deter potential conflict using the carrier, such as in a South China Sea or Taiwan crisis. It could, of course, also be used to support humanitarian and disaster relief missions. For regional contingencies, the anti-access capabilities that China currently possess offer more return for the investment, and some of these capabilities might be sacrificed if China pursues broader power projection goals centered on carriers.[38]

PLAN Training and Personnel Reforms

There is nothing particularly Chinese about the PLAN's ongoing efforts to simultaneously reform and standardise the way it conducts training and its impact on PLAN modernisation. Armed Forces, the world over, are tasked to train for the type of operations they will potentially be assigned to conduct. In other words, they must train the way they expect to fight. Over the last ten years the PLA's definition of the capabilities required for modern warfare has been repeatedly revised and updated.[39]

The PLAN issued revised training guidance to reflect these changes in the early 2000s. The Outline for Military Training and Evaluation (OMTE) was revised and reissued in 2001-2002 and then again in 2009. The PLAN's Training Regulations (TR) were revised in 2002. The OMTE is a compendium of documents which serve as the most basic guide to PLA training. They provide guidance on training goals, content, timing, as well as methods of quality control and assessment. Some of the key reforms to the TR included a new emphasis on training for officers and Non Commissioned Officers (NCOs). The 2002 PLAN OMTE called for command-track officers to focus on strategy, tactics, and innovation. To provide officers with the opportunity to focus on these issues, NCOs were assigned greater responsibilities for some tasks formerly performed by officers including overseeing training for new personnel; it also directed the navy to increase its use of simulators for training on new equipment and training combat methods, and to move away from scripted training events.[40]

Important changes to the 2002 TR included adopting training assessments as a factor for consideration in officer promotions, establishing procedures for integrating military academic research into operational training, codifying the required use of base training, simulator training, and network training. Finally, the regulations also included new content emphasising joint training, training for high-level headquarters, and non-combat operations.[41]

Two years after the PLAN's OMTE and TR were revised; President Hu Jintao issued the Historic Missions of the Armed Forces in the New Period of the New Century. The New Historic Missions tasked the PLAN to not only be prepared for the usual missions of deterring Taiwan independence and protecting China's maritime interests, but also to be prepared for safeguarding China's expanding economic interests including sea lane security and energy security. As a result of these new and expanded PLAN missions, the PLAN embarked to revise the OMTE to ensure that it was capable of fulfilling these new missions.[42]

The new OMTE came into force on 01 January 2009. New training objectives include focusing training on electromagnetic environments, focusing on training for specific missions and developing problem-solving skills, utilising military training coordination zones, and training for an expanding array of peacetime non-combat operations.[43]

New methods of officer commissioning reflected a paradigm shift in the PLAN's conception of modern warfare. The PLAN, like any other modern navy, required well educated officers who possessed good knowledge of science and technology and were endowed with diverse practical experience. In terms of this diverse experience, the PLAN assessed that officers should have both operational and managerial experience since such officers are likely to have a high degree of military professionalism, a well-developed ability to think strategically, and the competence to command forces in battle.[44]

New officers were commissioned into the PLAN through three routes: high-school students applying for admission to PLA academies, active-duty enlisted personnel applying to PLAN academies, and civilian college graduates. Traditionally, and up through the late 1990s, graduating from a military academy was by far the most common method of officer commissioning. Over the last decade this trend has begun to change and the PLAN currently inducts sixty percent of the officer corps as civilian college graduates.[45]

At present there are two paths into the PLAN for civilian college students. The first path is through the National Defence Scholarship program. National Defence Scholarship Students are recruited in high school or during their first year of college to study in a select number of Chinese civilian universities. As students, they receive a scholarship plus stipend, and complete some military training concurrent with their studies. Upon graduation they enter the PLAN as active-duty officers.[46]

As a relatively new program, the number of National Defence students entering the PLAN is continuing to grow. It has more than doubled from the 600 National Defence Students in 2006 to 1,250 from 2007 onwards. In addition to National Defence Students, PLAN on-campus recruiting offices also recruit from among the population of graduating seniors. Increasing PLAN training for nontraditional security missions is seen both as a means of protecting China's expanding maritime interests as well as sensitising regional countries to the PLAN's increasing operations at greater distances from Chinese waters.[47]

Endnote

[1] Cole Bernard D. The Great Wall at Sea: China's Navy Enters the Twenty-first Century, Annapolis: Naval Institute Press, 2001, p. 10.

[2] Ibid. p. 17.

[3] Ibid. p. 21.

[4] "People's Liberation Army Navy – History", available at http://www.globalsecurity.org/military/ world/china/plan-history.htm, accessed on 09 Dec 2010.

[5] Cole. op cit, p. 21.

[6] Ibid. p. 20.

[7] Joseph TD Gp Capt. Military Modernisation in China: Some Implications for India, Air Power Journal Vol 3 No 1 Spring 2006 (Jan-Mar), pp. 90-91.

[8] "People's Liberation Army Navy – History", available at http://www.globalsecurity.org/military/ world/china/plan-history.htm, accessed on 09 Dec 2010.

[9] Ibid.

[10] Ibid.

[11] Ibid.

[12] Shambaugh David. Modernizing China's Military, University of California Press, 2002, p 227.

[13] "People's Liberation Army Navy – History". op. cit.

[14] Ibid.

[15] Ibid.

[16] Ibid.

[17] Ibid.

[18] Ibid.

[19] Ibid.

[20] The Military Balance 2010. The International Institute for Strategic Studies. p. 377.

[21] Chinese Navy. Saunders Phillip C, Yung Christopher D, Swaine,Michael and Yang Andrew Nien-Dzu Yang (ed). O'Rourke Ronald, PLAN Force Structure: Submarines, Ships and Aircraft, p. 141. NDU Press, Washington DC, 2011.

[22] Ibid, pp, 141-142.

[23] PLA Armed Forces, Brahmand, Pentagon Press, 2012.

[24] Chinese Navy. op cit, p, 143.

[25] PLA Armed Forces. Ibid.

[26] Ibid.

[27] Ibid.

[28] China Year Book 2011. Singh Mandip, China's Military in 2011, IDSA, 2012. p 126.

[29] The force holding is based on inputs from various Chinese and Indian media and internet reports; list of forces, weapons and platforms is as given in Jane's Armed Forces 2011, The Military Balance 2011 and PLA Armed Forces, Brahmand 2011 as also an analysis of decommissioning and phasing out of older forces, weapons and platforms.

[30] Ibid.

[31] Wishik Anton II. Learning by Doing : The PLA Trains at Home and Abroad, Colloquium Brief, SSI, 2011. p, 2.

[32] Ibid.

[33] Ibid.

[34] Ibid.

[35] Cortez Cooper A. The PLA's New Historic Missions : Expanding Capabilities for a Re-emergent Maritime Power. RAND Corp, June 2009. p, 8.

[36] White Paper on China's National Defence in 2010 available at http:// english.gov.cn/official/ 2011 01/ 20/ content_1210227.htm, p. 47, accessed on 16 Nov 2011.

[37] Cortez, Ibid. p, 9.

[38] Ibid.

[39] Vellucci Frederic. Recent Trends in PLA Navy Training and Education, CNA, June 2009. p, 1-2.

[40] Ibid.

[41] Ibid.

[42] Ibid, p, 3.

[43] Ibid.

[44] Ibid, pp, 3-4.

[45] Ibid.

[46] Ibid.

[47] Ibid.

Chapter 4
PLAN's Quest for Seas Beyond China's Shores

"Whosoever commands the sea commands trade; whoever commands the trade of the world commands the riches of the world, and consequently the world itself."

...............*Sir Walter Raleigh*

Global interest and attention are increasingly turning towards the seas for a variety of reasons. Whilst the gradual resolution of conflicts on land, depletion of land resources and growing energy needs are contributory factors, it is the imperatives of globalisation and the extremely 'connected' world that are literally taking the world 'out to sea'.[1]

With maritime issues receiving greater attention in recent years, in stark contrast to clear land-oriented pre-occupations of the past, the varied dimensions of maritime security have indeed come into the limelight and assumed greater significance. This eventually influences naval force development plans of maritime nations.[2]

Unlike concepts of land power or air power, which are generally defined only in military terms, sea power can never be quite separated from its geo-economic purposes. Navies may be the palpable armed element of sea power, however, maritime shipping, seaport operations, shipbuilding industry, undersea resources, other forms of commerce and communications through fluid mediums are equally important and can all be seen as integral to a nation's sea power.[3]

Today, the world is increasingly being integrated through hyper-globalisation and the maritime dimension is gaining quantum importance because of the 70-80-90 concept[4], which is:-

(a) 70 percent of the world's surface is covered by the oceans.

(b) 80 percent the world's population is moving closer to the ocean littoral, and the majority of the world's major cities, industries and urban populations lie within 200 kilometers of the coast.

(c) 90 percent of international trade, by weight and volume, including most of the strategic cargo is carried over the oceans.

(d) Also, international law provides for freedom of the seas in which any nation can use the open ocean for purposes of trade or defense without infringement on another's sovereignty, subject, of course, to certain international agreements.

Sea Power is best leveraged by those who have the resources and will to use them effectively. While international law may provide for equal access to trade and resources, the means to defend such access against interdiction call for effective maritime forces. This has been the primary driving force behind the quest of nations for naval power.

The importance of a navy rests on twin pillars: its ability to influence events on land and its ability to control use of the sea. Technology has enhanced the reach and lethality of naval weapon systems which can now strike deep into enemy territories. The world's growing dependence on international trade and ocean resources has driven nations to build capability to 'control' ocean areas of interest. With this dependency in a globalised economic system, naval power assumes greater importance.

In the words of President Theodore Roosevelt in a 1902 address to Congress - "A good Navy is not a provocation to war. It is the surest guaranty of peace". Paradoxically however, the number of oceangoing navies has shrunk over the last decade. This process commenced with the disintegration of the Soviet Union. The United States continues to maintain a superpower-sized navy and some nations are quite satisfied with the evolution of this international system and see little political reason to maintain an oceangoing navy. For others, the economic cost of raising and maintaining a navy is simply unaffordable.

Traditionally, the roles of the navy have classified as - military, constabulary and diplomatic. In recent times, the benign role of the navy has assumed not only greater importance but also international acceptance as it addresses humanitarian aspects. With changes in the political and geo-strategic environment, a particular role assumes pre-eminence.[5]

This chapter attempts to provide an insight into the PLAN as a rapidly modernising maritime force, whose fleet over the next decade will be structured, equipped and trained for a diversified mission portfolio supporting China's expanding economic and military interests.[6] It shall go on to examine PLAN's Quest for Seas Beyond China's Shores through the former's aspirations and modernisation under the following:-

(a) China's naval modernisation strategy in the backdrop of its stated policies and guidelines.

(b) PLAN's missions and deployment patterns and the likely trends.

(c) Implications of PLAN modernisation and deployment for the region.

China's Naval Modernisation Strategy

In accordance with China's strategy for the PLAN's modernisation, the PLAN in the past couple of decades operated in accordance with the offshore active defence strategy.[7] This was to achieve an end state to win local wars under high tech conditions. This led PLAN to develop offensive capabilities to conduct limited sea control operations to enforce sovereignty and territorial claims in the East and South China Seas.[8] This requirement has changed slightly over the intervening years, to fighting and winning a "local war under informationised conditions".[9]

Further guidelines were formally delineated by President Hu Jintao in December 2004, in a speech on the "historical missions of the armed forces for the new stage in the new century."[10] These "historic missions" delineate the following four tasks for the PLA:-

(a) Consolidate the ruling status of the Communist Party.

(b) Help ensure China's sovereignty, territorial integrity, and domestic security in order to continue national development.

(c) Safeguard China's expanding national interests.

(d) Help maintain world peace.

As per China's 2008 white paper on national defence, China pursues a national defence policy which is purely defensive in nature. China places the protection of national sovereignty, security, territorial integrity, safeguarding of interests of national development and the interests of the Chinese people above all else. It goes on to add that the PLAN is a strategic service of the PLA and the main force for maritime operations. It is responsible for such tasks as safeguarding China's maritime security and maintaining the sovereignty of its territorial waters along with its maritime rights and interests.[11]

Much has been written and spoken about the Chinese defence budget, its opaqueness and the sizeable allocation to the PLAN. China's, like any other nation's, growing global economic reach and its consequent increase in military power are inextricably linked. National development is tied to global factors and expanding interests that demand increased defence capabilities.[12]

The two contradictions that can be seen however are the stated Chinese peaceful rise and the quantum of force and weapon acquisition and secondly the gap between China's stated aspirations and its present capability verses its force levels in the near future.[13] While some of us would like to or are coerced to believe that China aspires to oust US naval presence in her maritime vicinity or in areas that concern or comprise her core interests[14], my personnel opinion is otherwise. China is asserting herself like never before, but her current or envisaged near future maritime capabilities do not afford her the ability to operate credible maritime forces to power project in distant waters.

PLAN's Missions and Deployment Patterns and Likely Trends

China has decided to build and deploy apparently Asia's most diverse and capable naval force. PLAN commanders seek to realise the capabilities inherent in the party strategic guidelines over the next decade[15] by:-

(a) Becoming a viable strategic arm.

(b) Developing maritime strike packages to conduct and sustain "blue water" offensive naval combat operations out to the "first island chain".

(c) Providing combatants and support assets capable of limited force projection operations in distant seas beyond peripheral waters.

(d) Providing leadership, doctrine, tactics, and training for integration into joint and multinational operations.

China, as part of fulfilling its aspirations of becoming a world power has embarked on the path of augmenting its 'Comprehensive National Power' through political, economic, military, technological and diplomatic means.[16] As a means to the end, it is increasingly focusing on the waters that not only adjoin but also go way beyond her shores. This is in consonance with her quest for becoming a regional political economic and military power with global aspirations and an important player of the global strategic environment. China is conscious more than ever before that maritime trade, its security and naval supremacy will play a key role in its eminence as a global power.[17]

Towards achieving this ambition, the PLAN aims at a gradual extension of its strategic depth for offshore defensive operations and enhancing its capabilities in integrated maritime operations. This shift in its strategy has been necessitated primarily due to its trade and energy security concerns. Ensuring that its Sea Lines of Communication (SLOCs) remain open, safe and secure at all times has become an even more important Chinese maritime interest. These SLOCs stretch almost 9,600 kilometers from the Persian Gulf to the East Coast of China and currently transport 80 percent of China's energy imports.[18] This thus becomes the basis of China extending its maritime defensive perimeter and consequently improving its ability to influence and protect initially regional and subsequently global SLOCs.[19]

The latest deployment patterns of and the routes taken by the Chinese Flotilla seem to be in consonance with a three stage strategy in the PLAN's modernisation plans as indicated in the White Paper on China's National Defence. The Navy has been developing capabilities of conducting cooperation in distant waters and countering non-traditional security threats in order to progress the overall transformation of the service in consonance with its new strategy of far sea defence with long range capabilities.[20]

Through its three staged strategic transformation, the PLAN aims to further develop into a technologically modernised and networked naval force capable of operating within the first island chain comprising islands that stretch from Japan to the North, to Taiwan and the Philippines in the South. The second stage aims to transform the PLAN into a regional naval force that can operate beyond the first island chain to reach the second island chain that includes Guam, Indonesia and Australia. Finally in the third-stage, the PLAN seeks to transform itself into a global force capable of true blue water operations by the middle of the 21st century.[21]

Admiral Mike Mullen, chairman of the Joint Chiefs of Staff, said he was worried by China's "heavy investments" in sea and air capabilities. He added "A gap as wide as what seems to be forming between China's stated intent and its military programs leaves me more than curious about the end result. Indeed, I have moved from being curious to being genuinely concerned."[22] This probably is a sentiment that a lot of nations echo but may not say so in so many words.

With a presently limited capability in shore based maritime air and naval aviation capability, China has to necessarily rely on its missile armed submarines and shore and ship based Anti-Ship Missiles (ASMs) for control of waters in and around its shores.[23] This affords it the capability of pursuing a strategy of limited sea denial rather than outright sea control.[24] Even with its naval force build-up plans, it lacks the numbers to effectively deny over extended periods of time, areas like the South and East China Seas or the Yellow Sea. However, with its potent Anti-Access and Area Denial (A2/AD) strategy and its growing numbers of short and medium range ballistic and cruise missiles deployed on coastal and maritime units, China has slowly begun to flex its muscles not only in waters adjacent to her coast, but in those well beyond it as well.[25]

China's gradual aggressive posture has been made possible due to its bolstered capabilities in Anti-Ship Ballistic Missiles (ASBMs), Anti-Satellite (ASAT), reliable indigenous satellite navigation, high quality satellite imagery and Command Control Communications Computers Intelligence Surveillance and Reconnaissance (C[4]ISR).[26] Some of these capabilities are still unproven and untested fully, but their mere possession in an advanced stage of development have given China the much desired deterrent capability.

Chinese capabilities to conduct sea control operations further from its shores will become a reality if antiship ballistic missiles deploy and prove as effective and potent as many analysts fear, and PLAN submarines become increasingly capable of long, extended deployments.[27] PLAN's nuclear attack and ballistic missile submarines are deploying to new basing facilities in Hainan Island.[28] In addition to the aircraft carrier induction programme, the PLAN is in the process of inducting new classes of indigenous destroyers and frigates. These destroyers are designed to ameliorate the PLAN's most glaring maritime force projection shortfall namely the ship-borne area air defense and the capability to conduct long-range anti surface warfare missions with supersonic ASCMs. The PLAN's new frigates also incorporate much-improved fleet air defense systems and stealth design technology.[29]

The PLAN is also in the process of inducting a large number of fast-attack missile platforms with a stealthy, catamaran hull design. These will further bolster a range of missions in littoral warfare. Deployment of these vessels in swarm tactics as done by the Sri Lankan Navy in the Elam War could successfully support combat operations in a Taiwan theatre or a South China Sea conflict, as well as anti-access or area denial operations against US or allied forces.[30]

The PLAN anti piracy missions in the Gulf of Aden further demonstrates the seriousness with which Beijing views the security of its SLOCs. The Chinese task force has been operating far from home and that too for extended periods of time, putting its crew and ships under a lot of strain. Such considerations, off late, have led to calls for the establishment of overseas bases in East Africa, the Middle East and or South Asia.[31]

An important debate among security strategists concerns the protection of the Chinese trade and energy resources that flow through the Straits of Malacca and the South China Sea. While current and pending capabilities may allow China to negotiate from a position of strength regarding territorial and resource claims in the South China Sea, China has very limited ability to respond to large-scale threats to Chinese shipping in the Straits of Malacca and distant reaches of the South China Sea, leave alone the Gulf.[32]

China's thinking and slowly opening up its forward deployment[33] in order to showcase its naval presence in the Pacific and Indian Oceans from the hitherto South and East China Seas is a natural consequence of the country's desire to be a global maritime power. Modernisation apart, it has come to realise that naval power is more benign than land power. Navies by themselves cannot occupy or fortify areas at sea and thus must do far more than just fight. They need to protect not only trade and energy supplies, but also secure the routes and vessels that transit the same.

The incidents of harassment of United States Navy (USN) surveillance ships by Chinese fishing vessels in the South China Sea and Yellow Sea and the more recent incident with the Japanese Coast Guard illustrate what can be described as "strategic mistrust" based on inadequate military-to-military relations between China and the US and its other Asia and Asia Pacific maritime neighbours.[34]

Despite all indicators on China's maritime build up and modernisation my take on the same is that China has a long way to go in becoming a real maritime power. Maritime nations recognise that ships and submarines alone do not make for power. This argument can be carried forward in accordance with what Alfred Thayer Mahan defined as the essentials which determine the potential of a nation to become a maritime power.[35] The first essential was the requirement of a good number of ports and easy and unhindered access to the sea. In addition a two-coast configuration provided inherent advantages. Most importantly in order to be a truly credible maritime power, a country has to be able to dominate important SLOCs.[36]

While China comes good on two other of Mahan's stated criteria ie geography and population size, it comes a cropper as far as sea faring character of its people and its access to open seas is concerned. China's access to "open seas" can be constrained, in the North by Japan, in the centre by Taiwan and in the South by Philippines. The East and South China Sea SLOCs carry a considerable amount of global trade, especially energy. China does not dominate these SLOCs like India geographically does in the Indian Ocean Region (IOR) as also the energy lifelines from the Gulf.[37]

Implications of PLAN Modernisation

China's stated or otherwise naval build up and modernisation and its articulation of the South China Sea as a Core National Interest increases the complexity of the issue.[38] These could have a direct bearing not only on regional and global trade, but on its security as well. The Chinese envisaged A2/AD capability, if proven, could have far reaching security implications not only for the region but on the global front also.

Given China's unique interpretation of sovereignty in its maritime zones combined with a willingness to use force to support this stand is a destabilising factor for the security in the Asian region.[39] China is also displaying growing assertiveness in the pursuit of it's stated "core national interests".[40] The sustained emphasis on the modernisation of the PLAN without any accompanying transparency in its strategic goals also causes concern.[41] Though there has been some expectation that with China's growing power will come willingness for playing a greater role in global security and international order this is yet to be demonstrated.[42] On the other hand China's growing economic and military power appears to be making it more assertive as has been indicated by its apparent desire to divide the Pacific Ocean with the US.[43]

This aspect was echoed by many a Chinese scholar and PLA officers during the Xiangshan Forum that I attended in Beijing in end October 2010. Gen (Air Force) Ma Xiaotian while delivering the opening address at the forum stressed on China's peaceful rise and its commitment to peaceful development. He stressed on the fact that China's rejuvenation was in consonance with the "Tide of the Times". He added that China's military build up was to aid regional stability and world peace. He also brought out that China was the only big country in the world that was not fully unified. He stood by the Chinese belief that it was the country's policy rather than military strength that displayed its defensive nature. He, during his 40 minutes speech, repeated at least five times that China was not hegemonic in its policy, as believed by many nations around the world. He substantiated this by saying that China was the only country amongst the five permanent members of the UN that did not have any overseas military bases, nor had stationed any troops abroad.

Many Chinese PLA participants were of the firm view that China was neither a super power nor aspired to be one. They bluntly put it that China was not ready to shoulder international responsibility that accompanied super power status and added that as per their belief the word super power had a very negative connotation. Well so much for Chinese statements, their Chinese interpretation and subsequent denial.

The reverberation of China's economic rise and enhanced military capability is quite visible across Asia and as far as mainland US. Asian countries are responding to China's military might by building sufficient deterrence against possible escalation of disputes. Although several Southeast Asian militaries have security dialogues, military-technical cooperation and bilateral security arrangements with China, but are concerned about the growing Chinese assertiveness particularly in South China Sea. The South East Asian naval and air forces are miniscule both in terms of quality and quantity when compared with China's maritime forces and are urging the US to get engaged in regional security affairs much to the consternation of China.[44] They also seek cooperative agendas with India and Japan, the other major Asian powers, to contain China.[45]

As far as India is concerned, China does not appear to take India as a serious rival and underplays its standing by looking down upon its economic problems and inability to take on reforms in all fields. Chinese are critical of India's democratic process which has lead to a very poor pace of change but agree on the fact that perhaps this provides India a degree of stability which may see it through in an economic crisis where as China may not be able to do so in a similar case. China is keeping a close eye on India's growing political and economic sway especially in the Asian region. It considers strong India a challenge to its natural strategic space which it is endeavouring to carve out for itself not only in the entire Asian region, but beyond that as well. At present, outwardly, China reflects more concern about Japan, US and Taiwan and asserts that it wants to have peaceful and stable relations with its neighbours.

Conclusion

To conclude, it would be in order to say that reading too much into PLAN modernisation is going to serve no one well. Countries, which have the wherewith all and ability will continue to progress and modernise both economically as well as militarily. Aren't we doing this also? So why are we losing sleep over China's and more so PLAN's modernisation. The question we need to address is that over a long period will all these increasing numbers without much proven or visible capabilities and combat experience and demonstrated and well orchestrated war plans be sufficient or sustainable. China, while presently on a song, will soon have its own internal contradictions which will eventually get her to rethink on this feverish build up of capacity.[46]

In the long run whether this resolve will also easily translate into using maritime power to advantage of Chinese national interests is something that remains to be seen. A mere building up of platform numbers without demonstrated or tested fighting capability or a three ship extended period deployment or a ten ship foray within the first island chain or beyond without the ability to effectively control air space in the immediate vicinity does not translate into maritime power.[47] Therefore, while Chinese presence in seas beyond its shores is possible, it will not be credible, indeed, it will be counterproductive without any substantial maritime partnerships and involvement in any future security architecture in the region.[48]

Almost a century ago, Sir Julian Corbett warned "to aim at a standard of naval strength or a strategic distribution which would make our trade absolutely invulnerable is to march to economic ruin." He could not have said it better.

Endnotes

[1] Mehta Sureesh Admiral, Chief of the Naval Staff. In an address to the Defence Services Staff College, Wellington on 04 April 2008.

[2] Ibid.

[3] Ibid.

[4] Ibid.

[5] Integrated Headquarters of Ministry of Defence (Navy), Freedom to Use the Seas: India's Maritime Military Strategy, 2007, p. 71.

[6] United States DoD. Annual Report to Congress, "Military Power of the People's Republic of China 2009", p. 7.

[7] The PLA Navy: A Modern Navy with Chinese Characteristics, Office of Naval Intelligence Publication, Aug 2009, p. 7.

[8] Fisher Jr Richard D. China's Military Modernization, Praeger Security International, 2008, pp. 123-124,148.

[9] Thapliyal Sheru Maj Gen. PLA's New Mantra- Building Capabilities, AGNI Vol. XII. No III, p. 21. See also United States DoD. Annual Report to Congress, loc. cit, p. 11.

[10] The PLA Navy. op. cit, p. 7.

[11] White Paper on China's National Defence in 2008 available at http:// english.gov.cn/official/ 2009 01/ 20/ content_1210227.htm, pp.47,23-24, accessed on 16 Sep 2010.

[12] United States DoD. Annual Report to Congress, loc. cit, p. 32.

[13] Hayoun Jessie Ryou, "The Meaning of China's 'Peaceful Development' Concept, ORF Occasional Paper 12, Nov 2009, p. 2.

[14] Ranade Jayadeva. China's Recent Policy of Assertiveness, Centre for air Power Studies Issue Brief 34/10, 12 Nov 2010, p. 3.

[15] Cooper Cortez A. The PLA Navy's New Historic Missions. RAND Testimony CT 332, Jun 2009, p. 4, available at http://www.rand.org/pubs/testimonies/CT332/. Accessed on 09 Sep 2010.

[16] United States DoD. Annual Report to Congress, "Military Power of the People's Republic of China 2009", pp. 2-3.

[17] The PLA Navy. op. cit, pp. 5-7.

[18] Ibid.

[19] Ibid, pp. 9-11.

[20] White Paper on China's National Defence in 2008, pp.23-24.

[21] The PLA Navy. loc. cit.

[22] Admiral Mike Mullen, Chairman of the Joint Chiefs of Staff. Address to the Asia Society in Washington on 10 June 2010, available at http:// www.businessweek.com/news/2010-06-10/u-s-concern-over-china-military-growing-mullen-says-update1-.html accessed on 11 Jun 2010.

[23] Fisher Jr. op. cit, pp. 148-149, 189-190.

[24] The PLA Navy. op. cit, pp. 1-2.

[25] Pandey Dr. Sheo Nandan. Coping with the Rise of China: Imperatives for South Asia, ISPSW Journal, Jan 2011, p. 6, available at http://www.isn.ethz.ch/isn/Digital-Library/Publications/Detail /?id =125885, accessed on 05 Jan 2011.

[26] Cooper. op. cit, p. 2.

[27] Ibid, pp. 4-5.

[28] Fisher Jr. op. cit, p. 125.

[29] Ibid, pp. 148-152.

[30] Ibid, pp. 153-157.

[31] The PLA Navy. op. cit, p. 11.

[32] Ibid.

[33] Maj Gen Chen Yan. Commissar of the 5th Naval Escort Fleet Shares Stories at CRI, available at http://english.cri.cn/6909/2010/12/23/1361s611657.htm, accessed on 24 Dec 2010.

[34] Michael Mazza. Chess on the High Seas: Dangerous Times for US China Relations, AEI Newsletter No 3, Aug 2010, pp. 1-3.

[35] Premvir Das Vice Admiral (Retd). The Great Chinese Quest, available at http://www.business-standard.com /india/news/premvir-dasgreat-chinese-quest/399408/ accessed on 28 Jun 2010.

[36] Das. Ibid.

[37] Ibid.

[38] White Paper on China's National Defence in 2008, pp.23-24.

[39] Nagara Bunn. China's Strategic Culture and Current International Dynamics: Perspective From India, The Rise Of China, Pentagon Press and ORF, pp. 17-19.

[40] Swaine Michael D. China's Assertive Behaviour, China Leadership Monitor, No 34, Fall 2010, pp. 1-3.

[41] Ibid.

[42] Nagara. op. cit, p. 19.

[43] Cooper Cortez A. op. cit, pp. 4-5.

[44] Mearsheimer John. The Gathering Storm: China's Challenge to U.S. Power in Asia Fourth Annual Michael Hintze Lecture in International Security, 04 August 2010, pp. 2-4.

[45] Ross Robert S. The Rise of Chinese Power and Implications for Regional Security Order, Orbis, Foreign Policy Research Institute, Fall 2010, p. 525.

[46] Fisher Jr. op. cit, pp. 4-5.

[47] Das. loc. cit.

[48] Ibid.

Chapter 5
China's Maritime Strategy

China's Grand Strategy

There has been much debate about the rise of China since the early 1990s. This has generated a lot of concern in the international arena especially with respect to the pace of rise of China's economic and military capabilities; and how should the world, especially the Asia Pacific, respond to China emerging as a great power.[1] The dilemma faced by the world at large is that should states, contain or engage China.[2] Assessing the significance of China's growing capability and the advisability of alternative ways of responding to it, requires a grasp of the way leaders in Beijing seek to realise their nation's interests given the constraints imposed by their own resources and the international context within which they must operate.[3]

During the Cold War period, Beijing's overriding challenge was to ensure a relatively weak China's security in the face of pressing threats from the two superpowers.[4] The constraints of bipolarity resulted, first in alliance with the Soviets,[5] as a necessary counter to the perceived threat from the US and then,[6] after a fruitless effort to unite with the Third World in opposing both superpowers, in a security entente with the US to counter the perceived threat from the Soviets. Today, however, China has greater strength. It also believes that it faces few immediate threats. In addition to providing for core survival concerns, China's contemporary grand strategy is designed to engineer the country's rise to the status of a true great power that shapes, rather than simply responds to, the international system.[7] Achieving this goal, however, will take several decades of continued economic and military modernisation during which China must sustain its recently impressive record of growth. This Chinese ascent has caused a dramatic power transition within the international system, and more so in the Asia Pacific Region, which is also witness to dozens of outstanding and potentially dangerous territorial disputes.[8]

In the last few decades, the Chinese grand strategy has been to protect China from external threats as it pursues its geopolitical ascent. The purpose of this strategy has been to allow China to continue to reform its economy and thereby acquire comprehensive national power without having to deal with the impediments and distractions of security competition.[9] This strategy intends to give China the breathing room it needs to improve domestic social conditions, increase the legitimacy of the governing regime, expand the nation's economic and technological capabilities, strengthen its military, and enhance its standing and influence in the international political order; all of which are important elements in achieving its long-standing security objectives.[10]

In its policies toward the United States and other powers, the strategy aims to win support for China's expansion, while preventing any effort that may frustrate its growth.[11] To this end, the strategy focuses on developing and maintaining friendly relations with the major powers and convincing them that the rise of China will be a stabilising force in Asia.[12] By garnering this cooperation, the strategy aims to forestall a US defensive counter response that could widen the gap in power between China and the other major players. Continued friendly relations also improve China's access to the world's wealthiest economic markets.[13]

In its policies toward military modernisation, the strategy aims to reduce China's existing vulnerabilities while increasing the ability of its military forces to secure diplomatic and political leverage.[14] The modernisation in both nuclear and conventional forces is however going forward at a rapid pace, and has alarmed China's neighbours and major global powers.[15]

In its policies toward territorial claims, the strategy aims to avoid using force to settle territorial disputes.[16] Rather, it dictates that China pursue a good-neighbour policy designed to strengthen or mend ties with its neighbours and to delay resolving disputes, at least until the regional balance of power shifts in favour of China.[17]

In its policies toward international regimes, the strategy aims to secure advantages without incurring losses. Therefore, China's level of participation in international regimes in areas as economic development, trade, technology transfer, arms control, and environment, is determined on a case-by-case basis.[18]

History suggests that rising states tend neither to accept the prevailing global political order, nor peacefully integrate themselves into it. Nor, however, do they rush out to topple that order.[19] Rather, by asserting their new power, rising nations can precipitate a range of political, economic, and military tensions that draw the other world powers into conflict. Like other rising nations throughout history, a rising China is likely to assert its power.[20]

China's grand strategy is aimed at becoming a major power in the world and the Chinese debates indicate to "great power mentality". The implication of this policy is to firstly, tie-up with the United States as far as possible for enhancing China's comprehensive national power and wait for the gradual decline of the US. And secondly, marginalise any regional power, or, at an appropriate time in future, either make a tie-up or overcome any resistance for the leadership designs of China.[21]

If one of the medium term goals of China is to build a "well-off society" by 2020, China is likely to de-escalate on regional conflict situations, provided these do not affect its "core interests", such as Tibet and Taiwan. China's extension of this definition to include the South China Sea in 2009-10 has led to regional countries seeking US help and also engaging each other bilaterally to counter China.[22] It would not be wrong to conclude that it is China's exposure to the Pacific Rim and not her traditional continental influence over Asia that would be the avenue to whatever greatness China achieves towards the middle of this century. Indeed, maritime power has been cause and effect, as also the requirement and result of China's rise over the recent decades.[23]

This chapter will examine China's maritime strategy, as stated and demonstrated, and assess its compatibility with the doctrine of a peaceful rise, including potential intersections with other maritime powers of the Pacific and Indian Oceans.

Maritime Strategy and Maritime Power

The first work offering a scholarly look at sea power and its use in war was by Captain Alfred Thayer Mahan in 1890.[24] Mahan highlighted conditions which offered nations the opportunity to develop sea power, but focused on naval power's ability to win fleet on fleet action in the pursuit of national goals.[25] His contemporary Sir Julian Corbett provided more contexts for naval power, and thus a more convincing study of the contribution of sea power to national power: "Since men live upon the land and not upon the sea, great issues of nations at war have always been decided, except in the rarest cases, either by what your army can do against your enemy's territory and national life, or else by the fear of what the fleet makes it possible for your army to do."[26] Modern strategist Colin Gray linked sea power to national power in spheres beyond simply the clash of arms: "It has been no accident that from the defeat of Xerxes' invasion of Greece in 480-479 BC to the defeat of the Soviet Union in the Cold War of the late twentieth century, superior sea power has provided leverage critical for success in strategy and statecraft."[27]

Naval power in the strictly military sense is a key element of maritime power, influencing the diplomatic, informational and economic aspects. However, "All of a nation's maritime capabilities bear on its influence around the world and its ability to establish a peacetime presence at a point of choice."[28] Indeed, economic maritime power may be ascendant today, without resulting in colonial and imperial clashes at sea as in Mahan's and Corbett's time. This chapter will examine China's maritime trade, shipping, and shipbuilding, and the PLAN. First, though, it will define and discuss the theory of the peaceful rise, and then look at maritime thought and strategy and its place within the predominant strategic culture of China.

Ancient Chinese Continental and Maritime Culture

The People's Republic of China and its leaders trace their nation back 5,000 years.[29] Accounts of ancient China are more tradition than history: of the Xia, Shang, and Zhou dynasties, only the Zhou offers written records. The civilisation arose around the Yellow River, and to a lesser extent the Yangtze River.[30] Archaeological evidence of "...these ancient capitals testifies to the power of a kingship based on sedentary, landlocked agriculture and not on mobile, waterborne trade with other areas."[31] With the advent of Imperial China in 221 BC, as the Qin dynasty unified several warring kingdoms in North Central China, this continental focus continued. Once the canal systems were built, the rivers and the connecting canals provided transportation for people and grain.[32] With the addition of traditional fish farming the needs of the population were met by continental means.[33] The geography of the littoral area of Northeast China, on the other hand, was less suited to oceangoing, or even coastal transport. The coastline was largely reedy marshes. The harbours therein would silt and the land did not support forests that were suitable for shipbuilding. The barrenness and relative inaccessibility of the northern coasts resulted in the commonly held notion that the sea was nothing more than an uncommanded natural defence barrier. Thus ancient imperial courts ignored matters of naval and maritime speculation.[34]

Prior to the Qin dynasty unification, warfare focused on control of this non maritime land area. Although, Sun Tzu's Art of War and other military classics arose during these periods, they contributed little to a strategic maritime culture.[35] Additionally, any external threat to the Middle Kingdom came over land, from the North. Another factor that contributed to this maritime neglect was the rise of Confucianism. In the epic "Clash of Civilisations", Samuel Huntington goes on to classify China and other East Asian cultures as Confucian.[36] Confucianism contributed to China's overall culture, as also to a decline of maritime thought in the strategic culture by according a low fourth status in hierarchy to merchants, after the gentry, peasants, and artisans. Mandarins and other officials and the canal system bringing grain to the Imperial storehouses were important, but maritime trade was not.[37]

As the Chinese empire grew, the tribute system developed. From the Han dynasty (206 BC – 220 AD) onward, bordering tribes and states were encouraged to offer gifts to the emperor.[38] In return, the Chinese emperor would provide gifts of greater value. Eventually, this developed into a mutually beneficial security arrangement. The tribute system also developed into China's principal trade mechanism. Most of the tribute exchanges took place at the borders; goods and livestock were exchanged, and any other cross-border exchanges were forbidden.[39] For centuries, imperial China's strategic culture looked to the land borders on almost all political, military, and trade issues. That is not to say that no maritime culture developed. From the Eastern Jin Dynasty to the several Southern dynasties of the Southern and Northern Dynasties period, the lands South of the Yangtze were incorporated into the empire and settled by ethnic Chinese. The Qin-Han dynasties' incorporation of Guangzhou and Annam speaks to seafaring capability. But in terms of imperial attention, seafaring and maritime trade was not a focus.[40]

Between the eighth and eleventh centuries, with a larger population pressured by climate change, ethnic Han Chinese began migrating down the Yangtze River to the coast and then southward. The coastal tribes with which the Han then intermingled had not enjoyed the expanses of readily arable land of the Yellow and Yangtze rivers.[41] However, the coasts provided better natural harbours, and the coastal islands and mountain ranges did contain forests capable of supporting shipbuilding. During the Tang and Song dynasties, a maritime culture developed which differed from the continental culture of northern China.[42] Food production was not dominated by the centralised grain distribution system and fishing was coastal, rather than inland. Second, the coastal merchant was a key player in trade, rather than the primacy of the tribute system. Third, foreign influence and trade came into the coastal port cities.[43]

There is extensive evidence of Chinese sea trade with the Indian Ocean region, East Africa, the Red Sea and even the Persian Gulf.[44] Muslim traders complimented the Silk Road across Central Asia with this sea trade. Chinese trading junks travelled in the opposite direction, establishing coastal trade routes.[45] This maritime exploration flowered in the Ming dynasty with Admiral Zheng He.[46] The early Ming dynasty bore a familiar continental focus with consolidation of defences against the Mongols, and revitalisation of the Grand Canal, and re-establishment of the tribute system were high priorities.[47]

Between 1405 and 1433, Admiral Zheng He undertook seven expeditions, with around 317 ships and 30,000 sailors.[48] These expeditions went to all of the South China Sea, Sumatra, Java, and Borneo in what is now Indonesia; Thailand, the Indian subcontinent, East Africa, the Red Sea and the Strait of Hormuz.[49] They neutralised ethnic Chinese pirates in Sumatra, supported tributary states in regional disputes, established new tributary states, and traded goods.[50] Although Chinese merchant vessels had previously travelled these routes, but Admiral Zheng He's seven voyages reflected an unprecedented use of maritime power by the Chinese emperor. The Fleet projected national power to the end of their known world in support of national objectives, including trade, the tribute system, and a strategic outflanking of continental rival Tamerlane.[51]

This maritime focus was however short-lived. In 1411 the Grand Canal re-opened, and by 1415, coastal mariners were tasked to work on the Canal. Ship-building was turned to canal barges.[52] Construction of oceangoing ships was halted in 1436. A renewed Mongol threat brought the Ming court's focus back to continental defence. Finally, a newly ascendant school of neo-Confucianism resulted in a philosophical retreat from maritime expansion. By 1525 coastal officials were authorised to destroy all seagoing junks with more than two masts and arrest the crew.[53]

Continental focus would be the Chinese norm for centuries.[54] While imperial navies did exist, they were riverine or were used in haifang, or maritime defence. China was ill prepared when the threat of the eighteenth and nineteenth centuries came from the sea, in the form of European nations which were committed to maritime power as the path to national power. The 1842 Treaty of Nanjing ending the Opium War is an example.[55] This was the first in a series of unequal treaties that China would be forced into by unequal maritime power. Trade ports were opened, but imperial China would continue to administer them with the maritime superintendencies of the tributary system.[56] China recognised the imbalance of maritime power and undertook a program of naval self-strengthening, but the emphasis continued to mirror that of haifang, maritime defence of continental China. This would hold true through showdowns with the British, the French and the Russians until the disastrous naval defeat in the 1894-95 Sino-Japanese War.[57]

This strategic culture continued to hold sway through the Open Door period of European, American, and Japanese seeking trade privileges, naval shipbuilding contracts, and influence. Following the revolution of 1912 and abdication of the Qing dynasty, most of China's energies were directed internally, as warring factions attempted to consolidate control.[58] In terms of maritime focus, the situation looked very similar: the Navy and other maritime matters were a means of engaging with the maritime powers, but actually exercised little to no defence, as with Japan's advances in the 1930s.[59] After the war, the Navy continued to exist as an institution, capital was invested and it was a vehicle to engagement with Western nations. One highlight was the 1946 expedition to plant the flag on the Paracel and Spratly Islands. This operation of relatively short reach was essentially about protecting Chinese territory, not in extending maritime influence abroad. The next significant naval action was defecting to the Communist side in the spring of 1949.[60]

People's Republic of China's Strategic Maritime Culture

The strategic culture that developed in China can best be described as Mao Zedong's version of communism with Chinese characteristics. Some of these Chinese characteristics are emblematic of Imperial China, as "…the PRC is an empire in that it appropriates an imperial idea of China, reinventing a 2,500 year old autocracy to control its populace and hector non-Chinese neighbouring people."[61] The Chinese Communist Party may have replaced Confucian Mandate of Heaven with a more scientific mandate of history, but Mao's dealings with Khrushchev, Kissinger and Nixon at times resembled Imperial China's relationships with tributary states. The inherited characteristics include the continental nature as well as even the paragraph quoted above highlights that the PRC's desires for control were local, rather than global.[62] Mao Zedong thought does nothing to minimise the continental focus. First, Mao's version of Marxism-Leninism focuses on agrarian revolution and the rural peasant. Second in importance is the army, first the Red Army, and from 1949 the People's Liberation Army. These tenets drive a continental outlook.[63]

The nomenclature of the People's Liberation Army Navy reflects the relative importance of continental and maritime affairs. From 1949 on there was attention paid to maritime matters and to the Navy as there were maritime threats to the newly formed People's Republic, with the Nationalists occupying Taiwan and many offshore islands, and with the US Seventh Fleet operating in the region.[64] However, the PLAN was a defensive force, a continuation of the mindset that had existed since the late Ming Dynasty.[65]

Following the failed assault on Kinmen (Quemoy), PLAN coastal defence would closely resemble haifang.[66] Beyond the PLAN, the PRC worldview continued for decades to be more continental than maritime. The PRC's main focus was internal, but where it looked abroad, it was overwhelmingly aligned with the Soviet Union. This turned attention to the interior. While the early PRC may have acted aggressively in Korea and Vietnam, it did so only at its land borders.[67]

In 1960, Sino-Soviet relations suffered a split.[68] China's main foreign policy emphasis was to seek international leadership of the left, but the only maritime adventure of note at that time was the repair and training of Albania's ex-Soviet Whiskey class submarines. With border clashes with India and with the Soviets, the main external focus was continental.[69] Internally, the upheaval of the Cultural Revolution was loathed to the development of a strategic culture supporting a global maritime view. In the PLAN, politics trumped performance and professionalism. The PLAN's first political commissar, Admiral Su Zhenhua made an attempt to blend the Communist ideologue and the technical expert, but he did not measure up to the political ideals of the Cultural Revolution and he and the second political commissar, Vice Admiral Du Yide were purged.[70]

In July 1967, the Wuhan Military Region Commander General Chen Zaidao ordered PLA troops to move against leftists in Wuhan and the response included gunboats of the East Sea Fleet.[71] More purges of PLAN leadership at the same time seemed to have been directed against those unwilling to support the Red Guards. The most visible purge in the PLAN was that of Admiral Fang Qiang, who was in charge of naval construction and research and development. He was linked to head of state Liu Shaoqi. Chinese efforts to import Western shipbuilding technology were counter to self-sufficiency and emphasis on shipbuilding for maritime trade and economic interests in addition to being evidence of Liu's taking the capitalist road were a threat to the PLAN's defence against Imperialism. Shipbuilding, both naval and commercial felt an extensive political and technical impact.[72]

Following the Cultural Revolution and its failings, a number of elements began to align. The Soviet Union became the primary foe and China and the USSR fought a border war in 1969.[73] The Soviet naval threat was emphasised, and specifically their presence in the Indian Ocean. In foreign policy, the pragmatic Zhou Enlai began moving toward easing tension with the US. At the Fourth National People's Congress in 1975, Zhou Enlai introduced the Four Modernisations namely modernising agriculture, industry, science and technology, and national defence.[74] Following Zhou's and Mao's 1976 deaths, Deng Xiaoping took control of the party in 1978. At the 11th Party Congress in 1978, Deng formally launched the Four Modernisations, leading to an era of opening and reform. This opening and reform, especially as it leads to China's increasing integration into the world economy is the foundation to a new maritime beginning in Chinese history.[75]

Propounding of the Theory of Peaceful Rise

At the 2003 Bo'ao Forum for Asia, Zheng Bijian, the Chairman of China Reform Forum, and a longtime advisor to Chinese leadership, first described China's peaceful rise: China's development and the security of its 1.3 billion people required that China integrated with the global economy, fostered internal development without depending wholly on the international community, and adhered to peace without seeking hegemony.[76] Previous rises of new powers have disrupted the international system even to the extent of world war. "China's only choice is to strive to rise, and more important, to strive for a peaceful rise. That is to say, we have to work toward a peaceful international environment for the sake of our own development and at the same time safeguard world peace through this process of development."[77]

In December 2003, Premier Wen Jiabao used the term "peaceful rise" at Harvard University, adding official weight to Zheng's theory.[78] At Bo'ao Forum in April 2004, Zheng Bijian spoke again of "China's Peaceful Rise and Opportunities for the Asia-Pacific Region," while President Jiang Zemin changed the verbiage to "peaceful development."[79]

By 2005, Zheng Bijian wrote on the peaceful rise for Foreign Affairs with a change in emphasis. He drew a stronger difference between earlier plunder by rising powers, and China's emergence through peaceful means. While China's rise is rooted in self-reliance, it requires a hospitable international environment. Zheng spoke of "…a new international political and economic order…China's development depends on world peace – a peace that its development will in turn reinforce."[80] He went on to say that, "In fact Beijing wants Washington to play a positive role in the region's security as well as economic affairs."[81] Thus while China's peaceful rise may help safeguard world peace, it required some assurances from the United States as well. This additional emphasis was a natural outgrowth. Although Zheng's speech to the 2003 Bo'ao forum is often cited as the first full definition of the peaceful rise, he used the term in his speech at the Council on Foreign Relations and the Center for Strategic and International Studies, in December 2002. At that time, the Chinese leadership was attempting to counter a resurgence of Western concern regarding the China threat. Zheng portrayed China's peaceful rise as an opportunity for both China and the United States.[82] In doing so, he set the stage for the 2003-2005 formulation of the peaceful rise: China would continue on a path of development for its 1.3 billion people; this development could not be achieved without integration into the global economy; integration required a secure and stable international environment, while China would ultimately contribute positively to that secure and stable international environment, China required the existing great power, the United States, to allow economic integration and China's development. However, do the stated and demonstrated maritime strategies of China contribute to the secure and stable international environment? Or do they go beyond peaceful integration and constitute a legitimate threat to the international system and the United States?

China's Present Maritime Standing

Today China is integrated into the global economy in a big way. Because of the importance of maritime trade, China has become an important global maritime power.[83] As China's national interests take on an increasingly maritime focus, the development of a blue water navy is conducive to support its national interests. China's gross domestic product (GDP) in 2010 was $ 5.88 trillion.[84] China's exports in 2010 accounted for $1.581 trillion forming around 26 per cent of the GDP.[85] In addition to these exports, China's 2010 imports were $ 1.327 trillion.[86] Despite China's pre-existing continentalist tendencies, a look at China's trading partners indicates the importance of maritime trade.[87] At least 80 per cent of trade with its top ten partners is maritime.[88] China's reform and opening has led to a booming economy. But her booming economy leads to a requirement for maritime trade, for access to the international commons of SLOCs. China's maritime shipping industry has grown to meet the trade requirements of the economic rejuvenation. China Ocean Shipping Company (COSCO) was formed in 1961 with 25 ships and a capacity of 2,00,000 tons.[89] By 1978, China's tonnage was twelfth in the world, and by 2002, fourth in the world with an international ocean shipping fleet of 37 million Gross Registered Tonnage (GRT).[90] In 2010 China boasted of a fleet with 2010 vessels and a GRT of over 64.1 million DWT.[91] China also registered the highest growth world wide in yearly average tonnage during 2006-2010.[92]

China's shipbuilding industry ranks third in the world. A market share of approximately 20 per cent is a distant third to Japan and South Korea, but has been steadily growing. In addition to supporting the growth of China's merchant fleet, 90 per cent of the shipbuilding industry is to meet international orders, taking advantage of labour costs.[93] The shipbuilding industry and its advantage of labour costs is an example of one of the key drivers behind China's export growth and overall economic growth. As China's economy increasingly harnessed the productive capability of its population, it exceeded its capacity to power the growing industries. At the same time, urban centres, specially in coastal regions, grew exponentially, adding to the energy demand. China became a net importer of petroleum products in 1992 and of crude oil in 1993.[94] China is attempting to develop energy alternatives, and to find new resources in her own territories, but overall, dependence on oil imports is unlikely to change. Pipelines from Russia and from Central Asia are an important pillar of China's attempts to diversify oil transportation. By one estimate, pipelines could reduce China's oil imports by sea to around 70 per cent of its total oil imports by 2020.[95] In 2010 China imported 4.8 million barrels per day via ocean-going tankers. China's energy and economy are inescapably tied to the maritime domain.[96] China imports 47 per cent of its crude oil from the Middle East and 30 per cent from Africa.[97] Angola recently surpassed Saudi Arabia as the number one supplier of crude oil to China.[98]

China's state-owned oil companies are investing in Africa for exploration and production. In Angola, China outbid India's state-owned oil companies to acquire Shell's 50 percent stake in BP-operated Block 18.[99] China National Petroleum Corporation (CNPC) has invested over $8 billion in Sudan's oil sector. China National Offshore Oil Corporation (CNOOC) is the largest operator in Indonesia's offshore oil sector.[100] CNOOC spent $2.3 billion for a 45 percent stake in an offshore oil and gas field in Nigeria's Niger Delta.[101] CNOOC also has similar if smaller deals in Equatorial Guinea and Kenya. These newly acquired assets abroad provide about 8.5 per cent of China's imports, but they are indicative of China's continued pursuit of access to energy resources. All of these energy resources will come to China by the sea, and will require free passage through maritime chokepoints like the Strait of Malacca.[102] These efforts are more than just a natural outgrowth of energy resource needs. Much like Admiral Zheng He's trade routes that were active before and after his voyages, the significance goes beyond the activity itself. The significance is in the degree and extent of centralised, national commitment to the maritime domain.

Overall, however the increasing integration of China's growing economy with the global economy remains compatible with a peaceful rise. China's energy dependency is part of that integration. Direct competition for resources will almost certainly continue in the economic realm, but not in a clash of arms. As with other exports and imports, China's dependence on oil and other energy imports creates a virtuous cycle. While China's energy imports are particularly vulnerable to interruption at chokepoints, particularly the Strait of Malacca and the Strait of Hormuz, the dependency on imports creates a necessity for continued, peaceful, international access to the SLOCs of the Indian Ocean and the world. China has committed resources towards improved access to the maritime international commons. China has provided technical assistance, some 450 workers and as much as 80 per cent of the funding for the deep-water port of Gwadar in Baluchistan in southwest Pakistan.[103] China provided $198 million of $248 million for the first phase of the port's construction.[104] If expenditures on the second phase maintain that ratio, China could spend another $500 million in expanding the port to a dozen multi-purpose berths, a bulk cargo terminal, a grain terminal, and two oil terminals.[105] Beijing is also working with Myanmar in building or improving port facilities in conjunction with pipelines to Kunming to carry oil from the port facilities and natural gas from local fields.[106]

China's Maritime Strategy

Given Chinese opacity in general it is hard to hazard a guess as to: On what principles would China base its first-ever stated maritime strategy? The common denominator among the indicators of Beijing's intent explored above is the resolve to achieve China's interests on the high seas while avoiding armed conflict at almost all costs. No one wants a sea war, least of all China. Beijing's preference for "shaping," or creating favourable conditions in the strategic surroundings so as to achieve important goals without resorting to force, stems from the fact that armed conflict is risky, can squander resources needlessly, while even victorious war can provoke the vanquished into seeking vengeance, thereby perhaps undoing the victory.[107]

Sun Tzu, whose writings are a staple of Chinese strategic discourses, proclaims that the "acme of skill" is to win without fighting.[108] At the same time, Sun Tzu concedes that few attain such virtuosity. This necessitates the urgency for military preparedness both during wartime and peacetime. If combat readiness is the key to prevailing in war, perceived capability and skill represents the critical determinant of peacetime encounters.[109] By deploying military capability artfully to back up its words, the Chinese leadership can arrange matters so that rivals desist from challenging its policies or never oppose China in the first place. An obvious mismatch of power could dissuade adversaries and dishearten third parties that might be tempted to bandwagon against China. Words, capabilities, and deeds would let China win without fighting. The guiding logic is that people love a winner but will not place their bets on an obvious loser.[110]

Thus, peacetime clashes are head games. Scholar Edward Luttwak maintains that the outcome of peacetime crises at sea depends on how important stakeholders think a hypothetical trial of arms would have turned out.[111] This is why military analysts pore over the technical specifications of ships, aircraft, and armaments. They are attempting to glimpse the future. Convincing a prospective foe, that it would stand little chance in battle is central to prevailing in peacetime disputes. In short, whoever most people think would win in wartime, generally does in encounters short of war.[112]

PLAN Strategy Post Revolution

Naval strategy, operations and doctrines are changed according to capabilities that are possessed by a maritime power. Early on, PLAN was not sufficiently a modern force, primarily relying on Soviet weapons.[113] This greatly constrained the operational capabilities and goals of PLAN. But as PLAN modernised, its scope of operations and mission objectives broadened. The changing security environment and new emerging challenges changed the way in which PLAN was to assure its objectives. The PLAN in recent years has apparently developed doctrines for joint operations involving multiple military services, improved its military education and training and conducted more realistic exercises, and reformed its logistics system.[114]

Chinese naval strategists initially took the Soviet style of coastal defence.[115] It seemed practical and logical in the conditions of the Cold War. Soviet literature and many advisors were sent to China in order to train them in Soviet naval doctrine.[116] It had some relative success in stopping blockades, attacks on merchant and fishing vessels and functioned mainly as a defensive force. The PLAN therefore developed as a coastal defence force, with its primary mission being to prevent incursions from Taiwan and the United States.[117] During the Soviet threat, it played a largely supplementary role to the army. Deng's leadership and the span of General Liu Huaqing's command of the PLAN during 1982-87 brought navy back to its rightful place. General Liu had a tremendous impact on the overall naval strategy of China and redefined "offshore defence".[118]

This strategy included stubborn defence near the shore mobile warfare at sea, and surprise guerrilla like attacks. He emphasised on first line, second line and third line defence for the navy. The first line would include Yellow Sea, facing Korea and Japan, Western East China Sea, including Taiwan and the South China Sea.[119] These would be of vital national interests, with territorial claims, natural resources and coastal defence. The second line would be characterised by North-South line from the Kuriles through Japan, the Bonins, the Marianas, and the Carolines and mean control of all of East Asia. Third line would mean being a global force and having a global influence. Control over these first, second and third line defence should be achieved in 2000, 2020, and 2050 respectively. The long-range strategic objectives associated with China's potential long-term economic capabilities and great power aspirations such as the acquisition of extended sea control over maritime areas stretching as far into the Pacific Ocean, especially those regions described by Chinese naval strategists and leaders as the first and second island chains, do not determine current Chinese weapons acquisitions and modernisation programs in any direct, immediate and straight forward fashion, but rather the desired capabilities that Chinese force planners likely to aspire to incorporate into their force structure over the long term.[120]

The strategy in which a navy should ideally function is to affect the outcome on the land. So naval forces should be deployed to achieve a nation's objectives or guard a nation's interests.[121] China's many of the interests lie seaward optimising the use of navy. As explained above, major economic interests lay in the East and South China Sea. This required protecting important Sea Lines of Communication within this area. Second, are the disputes with many of neighbouring nations in all these areas, resulting in the demand of a formidable force, to influence the policy outcomes. Third is the Taiwan issue, where, it has to counter and deter the independence moves of Taiwan, and able to inflict some damage on the US naval forces from making inroads to the Chinese Seas. Fourth, it has to increase its influence in Indian Ocean, Arabian Sea. With current capabilities, sea-denial is well suited for the PLAN. Today China's order of battle boasts platforms well suited for sea denial, including sophisticated destroyers, submarines, ballistic and cruise missiles, and naval fighter/attack aircraft.[122]

Bernard D Cole brings in nine factors that would measure China's maritime strategy.[123] First, he says that 'training and education' are receiving importance, but 'suffer from time devoted to political education and resource limitations'. Second, the modernisation efforts are focused on 'naval systems and platform costs, capabilities and sustainability' but have 'resource limitations, relatively weak indigenous infrastructure and a low starting point'. Third, the scientific and industrial infrastructure is improving but 'inadequate to provide rapid design'. Fourth, 'the ability to derive doctrine and tactics is uncertain but clearly improving'. Fifth, administrational ability, command and control are improved to significant level, but 'uncertain in the fleet and theatre level'. Sixth, 'intelligence absorbs major resource of PLAN, but its influence is unclear'. Seventh, service-wide naval strategic planning is underway, but ignores on focusing on the adversary's strength. Eighth, national naval leadership is weaker and lastly naval strategists 'do not hold an enhanced position in the national-strategy making structure'.[124]

PLAN Strategy in the Twenty First Century

In 2004, PLAN Senior Captain Xu Qi published "Maritime Geo-strategy and the development of the Chinese Navy in the Early Twenty-First Century" in China Military Science, a leading Chinese defence journal.[125] He acknowledged China's historic maritime blind spot. The sea offered little but was viewed as an adequate barrier until the western powers invaded from that quarter.[126] In the last two decades, the collapse of the Soviet Union and the attacks of 9/11 provided historical opportunities for China's maritime geostrategic development. Simultaneously the geostrategic environment along China's borders had also improved.[127] China's economy and development, its key national interests, are inextricably linked to the seas. The main threat to China, the encircling hegemony of the United States, also comes from the sea. Development of a blue water navy and an ability to defend against a threat which occupies the open ocean is essential to China's long term national interests.[128]

The 2006 White Paper on China's National Defence[129] alludes to the peaceful rise and peaceful development in its foreword. The pledge of peaceful development is repeated in an introduction juxtaposing opportunity and challenges. On a global scale, hegemonism leads the list of challenges, but is not ascribed specifically to the United States. For China, "China's overall security remains sound…However, China's security still faces challenges which must not be neglected." The threat of Taiwan independence is cited as a grave threat to China's sovereignty as well as to regional peace. The White Paper on China's National Defence issued in 2004 identified the PLA Navy as a priority for development, along with the PLA Air Force and the Second Artillery.[130] This priority for development has been proven out by events. China has increased its surface combatant and submarine fleets, in both cases by both indigenous construction and purchases from abroad.

China's latest 2010 White Paper on National Defence published in March 2011 reiterates China's resolve to pursue a defensive policy, which it says is determined by China's development path, its fundamental aims, its foreign policy, and its historical and cultural traditions.[131] According to the paper this defensive policy is based on objective realities and its historical necessity. The road of peaceful development, adopted since 2006 in the place of peaceful rise is emphasised along with China's strive to build a harmonious socialist society internally, and a harmonious world externally on the principles of common security and prosperity.[132]

The White Paper for the first time has explored the issue of establishing mechanism of cross-strait military and security mutual trust. It lauds the progress in enhancing and building political mutual trust with Taiwan through a variety of agreements such as direct transport and trade links. It admits that the forces of independence in Taiwan, East Turkistan and Tibet have inflicted serious damage on China's national security and social stability. The paper goes on to add that Taiwan and China could discuss political relations in a special situation, and hold contacts and exchanges on military issues at an appropriate time and talk about a military security mechanism of mutual trust.[133]

The white paper sets four tasks for national defence which are as follows[134]:-

(a) Safeguarding national sovereignty, security and interests of national development.

(b) Maintaining social harmony and stability.

(c) Accelerating the modernisation of national defence and the armed forces.

(d) Maintaining world peace and stability.

The paper scripts out details of the modernisation of the PLA Navy which is seen to have evolved in accordance with the requirements of the stated offshore defence strategy. However, an enunciation of this "offshore defence strategy" is neither elaborated nor commented upon. The paper describes in detail as to how the PLA Navy is seeking new methods of logistics support for sustaining long-term maritime missions while continuing investment in a shore-based support system. It goes on to describe the notable improvement in the PLAN's capabilities of equipment support in long-distance and trans-regional manoeuvres, escort operations in distant waters and in a complex battlefield environment.[135]

The PLAN development shows an inarguable trend towards

development of blue-water capability. The PLAN is designed for the stated strategic goal of "active offshore defence." First announced in 1985, active offshore defence was a strategic paradigm shift from "coastal defence" which relegated the PLAN to a close-in role in support of a land war. Offshore defence involves maritime operations in aid of the following[136]:-

(a)   Keeping the enemy within limits and resist invasion from the sea.

(b)   Protection of the nation's territorial sovereignty.

(c)   Safeguarding the motherland's unity and maritime rights.

The second of these missions can be linked both to defence of continental China and to the sovereignty issue of Taiwan, as highlighted by the 2004, 2006, 2008 and 2010 Defence White Papers.[137] The acquisition of platforms and capabilities specific to denying US Navy access to the battle space in and around Taiwan has been a key focus of US concerns.[138] The evolution of PLAN definition of "offshore defence" in terms of all three missions highlights other sovereignty concerns. China has territorial disputes in the East China Sea, the Daiyou or Senkaku Islands, disputed with Japan and the South China Sea, the Xisha or Paracel Islands with Vietnam and the Nansha or Spratly Islands with Vietnam, the Philippines, Malaysia, and Brunei.[139] Admiral Liu Huaqing defined China's maritime defensive perimeter in terms of the First and Second Island Chains, which bound China's access to the Pacific Ocean and to the key chokepoints to the Indian Ocean. Senior Captain Xu, however notes that the United States has a system of bases and allies in the island chains, from South Korea and Japan in the North to the Philippines and Australia in the East.[140]

The First and Second Island Chains [141]

With China's development dependent on maritime trade, and more importantly imported energy resources, it can be argued that the First and Second Island Chains represent a barrier; an obstacle to overcome in defence of the nation.[142] Undoubtedly, China is developing capabilities to contest US Navy access to the battle space around Taiwan. Beyond a conflict over Taiwan, however, China's naval developments are compatible with the concept of a peaceful rise. China's naval diplomacy reflects the growth of the maritime dimension in national strategy. During the 1980s, China sent only two task groups to visit four countries.[143] During the 1990s, China sent 10 task groups to 20 countries.[144] Between January 2000 and 2010, 23 PLA Navy task groups' visited 46 countries.[145] This naval diplomacy has been tied to arms deals and to specific anniversary events, but overall, is in keeping with an increased global maritime profile and is not incompatible with a peaceful rise.[146] Similarly PLAN Commanders had never visited the Middle East and had visited Africa only once till the mid 1990s, have now been visiting almost every country the world over.[147]

China's Maritime Outlook

From Coastal to Offshore Defence

The change from coastal defence to 'offshore defence' has made PLAN function outside its coastal boundaries and become engaged in sea-denial and sea control activities.[148] There has already been a naval clash between the Vietnamese and Chinese over Spratly Islands.[149] PLAN has been slowly gaining control over the South China Sea. It has built an airbase on the Woody Island in the Paracels and also erected military structures in the Mischief Reef.[150] Japan and China have conflicting claims in Senkaku Islands where both countries have claimed sovereignty.[151] Japan's concerns centre not only on the territorial dispute over the Islands, but also on the potential threat to shipping lanes in East and Southeast Asia, and more generally on the consequences of possible Chinese regional hegemony.[152] Its strategic objectives would be to be able to tackle any contingency in terms of Taiwan, effective coastal defence, control of resources in the South China Sea and defence and deterrence against any sovereignty claims, protecting important SLOCs, acquire capabilities to deter other regional navies like India, Russia and Japan that could threaten its security.[153]

China's interest in the Indian Ocean is also seen in its attempts to build its presence in Myanmar, Srilanka, Bangladesh.[154] The Indian Ocean and the Persian Gulf are particularly important to China, not only for commercial reasons, but because those waters allow China to reach Iran, India, Pakistan and other nations of concern to its foreign policy. Its presence in the anti piracy patrol in the Gulf of Aden since 2009 is another indicator of its interests having reached the African shores.[155]

Diplomacy as a Means of Shaping the Maritime Environment

There exists a nexus among diplomacy, perceptions, and military capability. Diplomacy, defined roughly as the art of negotiating with foreign governments makes use of all of these implements to bolster diplomats' credibility vis-à-vis foreign interlocutors. The mix among these instruments depends on such variables as the strategic circumstances, the value each competitor attaches to its political aims, and thus the amount of resources it is prepared to expend on behalf of these aims and for how long.[156]

Diplomacy was the advance guard of the Chinese effort to shape the maritime environment in the near seas. Chinese diplomats rallied such legendary figures as Confucius and the Ming Dynasty Admiral Zheng He behind a charm offensive vis-à-vis fellow Asian powers.[157] During the 2008 Beijing Olympics opening ceremony, Chinese youth paraded images of these forefathers, in an apparent message that China was once a strong, seafaring nation that unlike predatory sea powers of the past refrained from abusing its neighbours, and that it was destined to follow this pattern as it regained its station among the great powers.[158]

The Chinese have mounted a sequential diplomatic campaign in the near seas over the past decade, adding each element of national power as it becomes available. Diplomacy is inexpensive.[159] Chinese diplomats could tell their nation's story how they wanted, even before China had amassed sufficient material power to put substance into their words. Economics came next, made possible by swift economic growth. By knitting itself into a tapestry of economic interdependence, Beijing furthered the narrative of China as a nation whose peaceful rise benefited all Asian states. Military power comes last, and indeed it remains an ongoing project. It is far from clear, for instance, that Beijing could enforce a "core interest" in the South

China Sea. At the very least, Chinese leaders would incur grave risk to interests elsewhere should they seek unquestioned primacy in any one theatre.[160]

Beijing appears to have misjudged the part military power should play in a maritime strategy that taps all sources of national strength. China's belligerence at sea over the past two years has squandered many of the gains it reaped from its shrewd diplomacy in previous years.[161] Its overemphasis on military force may be premature in any event. China cannot yet impose its will by force, while Asian powers have pushed back hard amid the recurring maritime confrontations with China thereby running the risk of uniting a hostile coalition.[162]

China's Take on Overseas Bases

China has refrained from setting up overseas military bases as part of Beijing's foreign policy emphasising non-alignment and non-interference in the internal affairs of other countries.[163] Chinese security analysts have often opined that forgoing overseas military bases was consistent with a defence policy that emphasised caution about entering into military alliances and deploying troops abroad. China's 1995 White Paper on Arms Control and Disarmament states, "China does not station any troops or set up any military bases in any foreign country".[164] Similarly, China's 1998 National Defence White Paper repeats this statement about refraining from establishing overseas bases.[165] China's 2000 National Defence White Paper also indicates that "China does not seek military expansion, nor does it station troops or set up military bases in any foreign country".[166]

PRC's growing global interests and its military's evolving missions are leading some Chinese analysts to suggest that Beijing may need to reconsider its traditional aversion to establishing overseas military facilities.[167] In particular, the PLAN experience with anti-piracy operations in the Gulf of Aden that began in December 2008 appears to have sparked a debate over the efficacy of continuing to adhere to China's oft-stated and long standing policy of refraining from establishing any overseas military bases or other dedicated facilities capable of supporting military operations in distant regions. This suggests China may be on the verge of moving beyond its traditional approach. Indeed, some Chinese scholars and military officers are now calling for the establishment of such overseas support facilities to handle the logistics required by a more active role abroad for the Chinese military.[168]

A radical departure from previous Chinese policy seems premature. Instead, statements by some Chinese scholars suggest that China may adopt a relatively cautious approach, which allows the PLA to more effectively carry out its new missions without requiring the formal alteration of Beijing's longstanding approach to foreign basing.[169] The most likely outcome is one in which China would follow an approach analogous to the "places not bases" strategy put forward by the US Pacific Command in the 1990s: establish facilities capable of supporting expanded PLA participation in non-traditional security missions such as anti-piracy and humanitarian assistance and disaster relief operations, rather than developing a network of traditional military bases, which would be extremely expensive, politically and diplomatically controversial and highly vulnerable in the event of a crisis or conflict. It is thus of interest that PLAN ships have visited Salalah Naval Base at least 23 times since establishing of the anti-piracy patrol.[170]

Aims of China's Maritime Strategy

The rapid rise of China has put forth many dilemmas in the minds of nation states. The primary one is whether to engage with China's power or to contain it? It is within the confines of the international system where nation states fight for political, economic and military space.[171] With its geo-strategic space in position, China has become a major contender for the various facets of space. What is more interesting is that, China feels that it is just and legitimate. It is further complicated by the fact that China gives such contradictory signs of being realist/pacifist, traditionalist/modernist, coercive/peace loving. Yet there are patterns that can be identified, which can be attributed to certain behaviour. This means, for a holistic part, it is necessary to understand the cultural dynamics of the state within inside and outside. China has been enjoying a geo-political centrality, highly hierarchical and socially defined society, with Confucian order, strong nationalistic appeal, and legitimacy of a leader that are all tied to the structure. Even as tremendous change has taken place, there are places where the country is bound by its culture, ethics, value-system, national cohesion etc.[172]

China's thirst for great power status, its strong feeling for the unification,

Sino-centric order, can all be attributed to its past influences.[173] As China grows, these aspirations will be carried out by the Chinese Communist Party, proving its legitimacy and control to its people. Its resources, political, economic and military would be utilised towards achieving the end state as envisioned by its grand strategy. Today, China's growth can be seen in all sectors and has had a spiraling effect on its stature and place in the international system.[174]

One of the determining factors that would set the tone for future is the reunification of Taiwan. This is the core challenge and an objective of every successive leader of the CCP.[175] The conflict has the potential to bring in great powers, and the role of United States would be decisive factor in affecting the overall nature of the conflict. The only feature that is stopping the PRC to forcibly unite is the threat of intervention by the United States.[176] So the PRC is increasing its capabilities in military, especially in the maritime sector. It wants to increase the regional military dynamics in its favour. As its military power grows, the hesitation to use force would decrease. China would want to increase its influence in the Asia Pacific region, and slowly expand into the Indian Ocean region, guarding its important SLOCs, influencing critical policy structure of countries, fully utilising its resources and guaranteeing uninterrupted energy and resource flow to its shores.[177] Finally it would desire a multilateral world order, where China would not impose, but influence a just power relation and end US hegemony in the Asian region and to achieve its great power status.[178]

While China's economy is on a roll, there are certain issues in its fiscal and banking sector. Also the governance level at the provincial level is poor, and state institutions such as the judiciary and police are not known to be people oriented, and could cause social upheaval. Another cause for concern is as the economy grows, there is an increasing stress on the environment and can cause challenges in crop production, usage of water and health issues. Also the urban-rural divide is growing. There have been more than 50,000 protests in the rural areas;[179] which have been quelled with force and many have gone unreported. So the government's main challenge would be to continue to make the economy grow, increase the country's wealth accumulation and increase the nation's comprehensive national power.[180]

Second, the modernisation process in the military will enable it to meet security challenges as well as project power. The military would also play an important role in achieving its foreign policy goals. Towards this end, the modernisation of the PLAN has received additional attention, as China's interests increasingly turn sea based.[181]

Overall China's maritime strategy would aim to achieve certain specific short term and long-term goals. China's economy will continue to fund such military projects for its territorial defence, offshore defence and also improving its overall deterrence. Although realisation of its goals might be years away, the investment in PLAN appears to target the sort of capabilities that would enable China to play the role of a great maritime power that it once was.[182] The primary aims of the Chinese maritime strategy could be summarised as follows[183]:-

(a) **Re-unification of Taiwan**. Re-unification with Taiwan remains the most important strategic goal of the PRC. The PRC's attempts to intimidate the Republic of China (ROC) government in Taiwan, provides an example of how China is already using its armed forces at well-chosen times to accomplish its grand strategic goals. The PLAN holds annual exercises of naval manoeuvres of a very grand scale, designed to simulate a naval confrontation in the Taiwan Straits followed by a marine invasion of Taiwan. With the recent economic overtures like the Economic Cooperation Framework Agreement (ECFA), China is attempting to integrate the ROC economically as well.[184]

(b) **Diminish US Supremacy in the Asia Pacific**. Chinese grand strategy also facilitates to dethrone US from its supremacy in the Asia Pacific. This would not only afford China strategic space therein, but also establish it a key global maritime player. The PLAN with its asymmetric capabilities would play a bigger role in erasing that supremacy. The realisation that without sea power, the domination of the land is not possible is being fast recognised by the Chinese. So starting from East Asia, South Asia, to the Indian Ocean and the Arabian Sea, the influence and presence of the PLAN is growing, causing concern not only for the US, but for regional navies' as well.[185]

(c) **Secure SLOCs and Protect Assets Offshore**. A long term strategic goal of the Chinese through the PLAN is to dominate and protect its SLOCs not only in the region, but the world over. This is vital to ensure uninterrupted supply lines of the resource and energy hungry China. Protection of offshore assets, claims over disputed territories and safety of assets on foreign soil would require the PLAN to extend its influence and project power much beyond its coastal areas.[186]

Implications of China's Maritime Strategy for India

While in public, India may speak warmly about China, but deep within there is a growing concern about China's assertiveness and its willingness to use force.[187] The Asia Pacific region which is home to the world's two oldest civilisations, is also witness to dozens of outstanding and potentially dangerous territorial disputes.[188] This region could also become an arena for the new cold war with an emerging and consequently assertive China taking head-on the sole superpower; the USA, now somewhat weary and over-stretched with its global commitments and interventions in Iraq and Afghanistan.[189] Some analysts feel that the world's maritime future is likely to be determined in large measure in the Asia Pacific, particularly by the developing relationship between the maritime powers of the region.[190]

Global affairs today are traversing through a period of instability. The reason for this instability lies in the transition of global power that is currently underway. The two poles to this transition are the relative decline of the United States and the rise of China.[191] While the US's relative decline has been a long and slow process, the evident and more dramatic rise of China over the last two decades, is going to impact not just its neighbours in the Asia Pacific, but the entire world.[192] History has shown us that great powers will always seek to dominate their neighbourhood and as much of the rest of the world as they can. There is nothing peculiarly Chinese about it.[193] But the obverse is equally true. The rise of the Asia Pacific giants ie India and China, is likely to be as problematic, tense and destabilising as that of any other powers.[194] Certain concerns that are peculiar to India are as follows:-

(a) **China's Military Build-up and PLAN Presence in the Indian Ocean.**[195] In recent years China's defence budget has grown at more than 10 per cent a year, while the Indian defence budget has grown at a much lower rate. China has managed to keep three or more warships off the coast of Somalia for the past two years, as part of the international anti-piracy effort, revealing considerable logistical strength. It is building commercial ports along the shores of the Indian Ocean in Myanmar, Pakistan, Sri Lanka and elsewhere. Some Indians worry that the ports could have a military use. The Chinese say they need to be in the Indian Ocean to secure supply routes for imports of oil and raw materials. In Tibet, China has built roads, railways and airports, which could serve as a launch pad for a potential attack on India. The Indians are belatedly trying to improve infrastructure on their side of the border.

(b) **Chinese Con-circlement of India.**[196]   China has forged warm relations with many of India's neighbours, such as Bangladesh, Myanmar, Nepal, Pakistan and Sri Lanka. Some Indian strategists worry about being surrounded by countries that have entered China's orbit. In Nepal, China has good relations with the Maoists, who are the most powerful force in that unstable country. China is the dominant power in Myanmar, where it is building pipelines to transport oil and gas from the Bay of Bengal to the province of Yunnan.[197] China has invested massively in Sri Lanka, constructing ports, roads, power plants and airports. Last year China was Sri Lanka's biggest donor, providing $1.2 billion of aid.[198] It is also the country's main supplier of weapons. China and Pakistan have a longstanding diplomatic and military alliance. India believes that Beijing is still giving Islamabad direct assistance with its nuclear weapons programme.[199]

(c) **China's Successful Natural Resource Diplomacy.**[200] Both, India and China, rely heavily on imported hydrocarbons and other raw materials to fulfill their ever growing hunger for energy and natural resources. Indians often compete against the Chinese for access to natural resources in Central Asia, Latin America and Africa. China tends to win contracts against Indian competition because its state owned firms are prepared to pay over the market price, while Indian companies struggle with bureaucratic and procedural delays. In 2010 Chinese companies spent $32 billion acquiring energy and resources assets overseas, against a single $2.1 billion investment by India's Oil and Natural Gas Corporation.[201]

(d) **Trade Imbalance**.[202] Although Sino-Indian commerce is booming, it is unbalanced and tilted in China's favour. China enjoyed a large trade surplus, worth $26 billion in 2010.[203] India exports mainly raw materials, such as iron ore, while it imports Chinese manufactured goods. The Indians concern about China's undervaluation of the Yuan explains part of the deficit.[204]

Indian Response to China's Rise

The Indian response to China's rise is best brought out in pursuing a two-pronged strategy. The first prong is to reinforce India's internal strength, by boosting economic growth, including through the development of closer economic ties with China, and by tackling both terrorism and separatism. In the long run China will have to show more respect for a strong India.[205]

The second prong is to develop a set of alliances and relationships that will reduce the potential threat from China. India needs to build a web of close ties with other countries that worry about China's ascendancy. India's armed forces enjoy warm relations with those in Vietnam, Singapore, the Philippines and Indonesia.[206] There is an increasingly intimate relationship with Japan, which is now a big investor in Indian infrastructure. India holds naval exercises with Japan and the US. Some Indian strategists are open to the idea of reviving the 'quadrilateral initiative';[207] in 2007 this informal grouping of the US, India, Japan and Australia led to discussions on security, as well as naval exercises in the Bay of Bengal.[208] But when China made a fuss about the grouping a couple of years ago, Australia pulled out and the initiative faltered. The American strategy for dealing with China can be described as 'engage and hedge', engage with China, to promote greater contact, particularly in the economic sphere; but hedge against the risk of it turning nasty by building alliances with others who have worries about China. For the foreseeable future India's own strategy needs to be very similar.[209]

Since both India and China are rising powers in the same part of the world, there is bound to be friction between them.[210] Several South East Asian countries are becoming closely connected to China and they may well be incapable of standing up to it on an important issue.[211] Although India worries more about China than China does about India, China has more expertise on India than vice versa.[212]

India continues to have a poor record of befriending its immediate neighbours.[213] Till such time India fails to implement policies that make economic co-operation attractive to our neighbours, Chinese economic penetration of South Asia will continue unimpeded."[214] The lack of economic integration in South Asia is extraordinary. Only 5 per cent of South Asian countries' exports go to the region. Poor infrastructure that raises transport costs, cumbersome border procedures, enmity between governments, non-tariff barriers and high tariffs have all smothered trade.[215]

The South Asian Association for Regional Cooperation (SAARC) has achieved very little.[216] India should take the lead in trying to remove barriers to trade, and as the region's economic giant lower barriers more quickly than its neighbours.

India should take a lesson in managing its neighbourhood from Beijing: in recent years, China has solved land border disputes with all its neighbours except India, offered them preferential trade terms, and made large investments in infrastructure that will encourage commerce such as building roads into Nepal and pipelines into Turkmenistan. In the words of one Indian government official: "The best response to the rise of China is the rise of India."[217] India is rising, driven by strong economic growth, likely to be more than 8 per cent this year.[218] One big difference between India and China, of course, is their political systems. Chinese officials are not envious of India's democracy.[219] One reason for their disdain towards India is that they think its decentralised and often chaotic political system creates inefficiencies that hamper economic growth.[220] The continuing rise of India requires not only strong growth, but also clever diplomacy. India has done well to build friendships with the US, Japan and many South East Asian states. But it needs to improve its performance in its neighbourhood.[221]

India is furthering its 'Look East' policy articulated two decades ago with renewed gusto.[222] Look East mainly envisages expanding economic and political ties in Southeast Asia, but it does not rule out military engagement therein. The 2007 Indian Maritime Strategy designates the northern Indian Ocean, the Persian Gulf and the SLOCs therein as 'primary areas' of interest and the South China Sea, Southern Indian Ocean Region, the Red Sea and the East Pacific Region as 'secondary areas' for the exercise of sea power. The areas of secondary interest, will come in where there is a direct connection with areas of primary interest, or where they impinge on the deployment of future maritime forces.[223] The South China Sea meets both tests. It adjoins primary zones of interest in the Malacca Strait and the Bay of Bengal. And Chinese efforts to enforce its maritime claims vis-à-vis other navies would clearly influence how India deploys seagoing forces in Southeast Asia.[224] The next encounter on the high seas may well involve real warships on both sides.[225]

Endnotes

[1] Mishra Brajesh. Keynote Address, China's Quest for Global Dominance: Reality or Myth. Ed Sandhu Maj Gen PJS. Vij Books India Pvt Ltd, New Delhi. p. 4.

[2] Ibid. p. 5.

[3] Prabhakar W Lawrence S. China's Strategic Culture and Current International Dynamics: Perspective From India, The Rise Of China, Pentagon Press and ORF, p. 37. Tellis Ashley, Dr. China's Grand Strategy, China's Quest for Global Dominance: Reality or Myth. Ed Sandhu Maj Gen PJS. Vij Books India Pvt Ltd, New Delhi. p. 28.

[4] The PLA Navy: A Modern Navy with Chinese Characteristics, Office of Naval Intelligence Publication, Aug 2009, p. 4.

[5] Cole Bernard D. The Great Wall at Sea: China's Navy Enters the Twenty-first Century, Annapolis: Naval Institute Press, 2001, p. 20.

[6] Shambaugh David. Modernizing China's Military, University of California Press, 2002, p. 307.

[7] Rigby Richard, Dr. China's Grand Strategy, China's Quest for Global Dominance: Reality or Myth. Ed Sandhu Maj Gen PJS. Vij Books India Pvt Ltd, New Delhi. p. 32.

8 Bisley Nick. Building Asia's Security. International Institute for Strategic Studies, Routledge, 2009. pp. 9-11.

9 Swaine Michael D and Tellis Ashley J. Interpreting China's Grand Strategy : Past, Present and Future. RAND Research Brief. MR-1121-AF, 2000. pp. 10-11. United States DoD. Annual Report to Congress, "Military Power of the People's Republic of China 2009", pp. 2-3.

10 Ibid.

11 Swaine Michael D. op cit. United States DoD. Annual Report to Congress, "Military and Security Developments Involving the People's Republic of China 2011", p. 9.

12 Ibid.

13 Swaine Michael D. op cit. United States DoD. 2011. p. 13.

14 Ibid. United States DoD. 2011. pp. 14, 22.

15 Swaine Michael D. op cit. Mohan Raja C. Power and Paradox: The Future of Sino-Indian Relations, Think India Quarterly, Vol13, No 2, Apr-Jun 2010, p. 207. Ibid. p.14.

16 Swaine Michael D. op cit. United States DoD. op cit. pp. 14-15.

17 Swaine Michael D. op cit. Subrahmanyam K. Countering China's New Assertiveness available at http://business-standard.com/ india/ storypage.php?autono=406992 accessed on 07 Sep 2010.

18 Swaine Michael D. op cit.

19 Swaine Michael D. op cit.Mishra Brajesh. op cit. p. 5.

20 Ibid.

21 United States DoD. Annual Report to Congress, "Military Power of the People's Republic of China 2009", pp. 2-3.

22 United States DoD 2011. op cit. pp. 2, 7.

23 Ibid. p. 57.

24 Premvir Das Admiral. The Great Chinese Quest, available at http://www.business-standard.com /india/news/premvir-dasgreat-chinese-quest/399408/ accessed on 28 Jun 2010.

25 Ibid.

26 Corbett Julian S, Some Principles of Maritime Strategy, Naval Institute Press, Annapolis, 1988), p. 16.

27 Gray Colin S, The Leverage of Sea Power, The Free Press, New York, 1992. p.ix.

28 Integrated Headquarters of Ministry of Defence (Navy), Freedom to Use the Seas: India's Maritime Military Strategy, 2007, pp. 3-7.

[29] Shaughnessy Edward L. China: Empire and Civilization, Oxford University Press, 2000, p 27.

[30] Ibid.

[31] Levathes Louise. When China Ruled the Seas, Oxford University Press, 1994, p 32. Fairbank John King and Goldman Merle, China: A New History, Cambridge, MA, Harvard University Press, 1996. p. 35.

[32] Mote FW. Imperial China, Harvard University Press, 1999, pp. 646-647.

[33] Nodskov Kim. The Long March to Power. Royal Danish Defence College Publishing House, 2009, p 27. The focus of a continental power lies on the continental landmass. Its concerns centre on developing large land forces capable of securing its borders and establishing and protecting buffers to ensure external security. In contrast, a maritime state has its interests centered on overseas trade, possessions and dependencies. It also typically possesses a strong merchant class, a large merchant marine and a navy capable of controlling surrounding home waters as well as oceanic trade routes. Swanson Bruce. Eighth Voyage of the Dragon: A History of China's Quest for Sea power. Annapolis: Naval Institute Press, 1982, pp.206-211, 224-245.

[34] Mote FW. op cit, pp. 719-720. Swanson Bruce. Ibid.

[35] Ibid.

[36] Huntington Samuel P, The Clash of Civilizations and the Remaking of World Order. New York: Touchstone, 1996. Huntington introduces the idea of a "Sinic" culture of China, Chinese in Southeast Asia, and "the related cultures of Vietnam and Korea." pp. 45-47.

[37] Levathes Louise. loc cit. p 32. Swanson Bruce. loc cit. p. 15.

[38] Shaughnessy Edward. loc cit.

[39] Swanson Bruce, loc cit. p. 15.

[40] Fairbank John King and Goldman Merle. loc cit. p. 190.

[41] Levathes Louise. loc cit.

[42] Levathes Louise. op. cit, p. 49.

[43] Ibid, p 42. Swanson Bruce. loc cit. pp. 17-18.

[44] Levathes Louise. Ibid. pp.32-35.

[45] Ibid.

[46] Ibid. p. 21.

[47] Ibid.

[48] Ibid. p. 82.

[49] Ibid.

[50] Ibid.

[51] Ibid. p. 21.

[52] Ibid, pp 174-175. There are numerous factors which contributed to the decline of the early Ming Navy. One explanation is that the voyages were stopped by Confucian-trained scholar-officials who opposed trade and foreign contact. A second explanation is the loss of revenue and prestige associated with efforts to quell rebellion in Annam (North Vietnam). In 1420, the Ming Navy was defeated by Annamese rebels at the Red River. This was the first of a series of setbacks which resulted in the evacuation of Tonkin in 1428. A third explanation is the revival of Mongol power in the Northwest, which became the total preoccupation of the Ming court. A final explanation is the reopening of the Grand Canal in 1411 and the disbandment of the grain transportation fleet in 1412, which destroyed the basis of naval mobilisation of ships and trained men. This, combined with the fixation on security in the Northwest, opened the coastline for predation by Japanese based pirates. The response of the Ming court was to remove the population from coastal areas rather than to confront the pirates at sea.

[53] Hsu Immanuel CY. The Rise of Modern China. Oxford University Press, 2000. pp. 192-193. Swanson Bruce. loc cit. pp.28-40.

[54] Nodskov Kim. loc cit.

[55] Hsu Immanuel CY. op cit.

[56] Levathes Louise. loc cit. p. 21.

[57] Hsu Immanuel CY. op cit. pp. 342-345.

[58] Mote FW. op cit, pp. 646-647.

[59] Hsu Immanuel CY. op cit. pp. 583,587.

[60] Ibid. p 623.

[61] Terrill Ross. The New Chinese Empire. Basic Books. New York. 2003. p. 3.

[62] Ibid. pp. 4-8.

[63] The Chinese economy was too weak to sustain the investment necessary to develop an ocean-going fleet. Moreover, it was inconceivable that China could have developed sufficient naval power to challenge the US for control of East Asian waters.

[64] The PLA Navy. op cit, p. 4.

[65] Shambaugh David. loc cit.

[66] Swanson Bruce, loc cit. pp. 183-215

[67] Ibid.

[68] Shambaugh David. op. cit, p 227.

[69] Terrill Ross. loc cit. pp. 258-261.

[70] Shambaugh David. op. cit, pp. 112-114.

[71] Fisher Jr Richard D. China's Military Modernization, Praeger Security International, 2008, p 69.

[72] The PLA Navy. op. cit. p.5. Swanson Bruce. loc cit. pp. 237-244.

[73] Swanson Bruce. op cit.

[74] Muller David G. China as a Maritime Power. Boulder, Westview Press, 1983. pp.145-155, 179-195.

[75] Shambaugh David. op. cit, p 192.

[76] The PLA Navy. op. cit, p. 7.

[77] Bijian Zheng, "A New Path for China's Peaceful Rise and the Future of Asia," speech to the Bo'ao forum for Asia, April 2003, reproduced in China's Peaceful Rise: Speeches of Zheng Bijian 1997-2005. Brookings Institution Press. Washington DC. 2005. p. 18.

[78] Jiabao Wen, "Turning Your Eyes to China," speech on 10 December 2003, transcript available in the Harvard Gazette Archives. available at http://www.hno.harvard.edu/gazette/2003/12.11/10-wenspeech. Html. Accessed on 05 March 2011.

[79] Guo Sujian. "Challenges and Opportunities for China's 'Peaceful Rise'," in China's Peaceful Rise in the 21st Century: Domestic and International Conditions, ed. Sujian Guo. Ashgate, Aldershot, 2006. pp. 1-14.

[80] Bijian Zheng. "China's Peaceful Rise to Great-Power Status." Foreign Affairs 84, September/October 2005. p. 24.

[81] Ibid.

[82] Bijian Zheng. loc cit. pp. 67-73.

[83] Prabhakar W Lawrence. loc cit. p. 37.

[84] Economy of the People's Republic of China. Available at http://en.wikipedia.org/wiki/Economy_ of_the_ People's_Republic_of_China. Accessed on 20 August 2011. pp. 1-2.

[85] Ibid.

[86] Ibid.

[87] Weijie Gao, "Development Strategy of Chinese Shipping Company under the Multilateral Framework of WTO" speech to the International Maritime Forum 2003, Available at http://www.cosco.com.cn/ en/pic/forum/654923323232.pdf. accessed on 20 August 2011.

[88] Ibid.

[89] China Analysis Brief. Available at http://www.eia.gov/EMEU/cabs/China/pdf.pdf. Accessed on 27 August 2011. pp. 1-4.

[90] Ibid.

[91] Ibid.

[92] Ibid.

[93] Economy of the People's Republic of China. op cit. pp. 20-22.

[94] China Analysis Brief. op cit.

[95] China-CNPC, China-Myanmar Oil & Gas Pipeline. Project report available at http://www.cceec.com.cn/ English/Project/China/2010/0914/8530.html, accessed on 12 Aug 2011. Herberg Mikkal E. Pipeline Politics in Asia. NBR Special Report 23, Sept 2010. pp. 3-6.

[96] China Analysis Brief. op cit.

[97] Ibid.

[98] Ibid.

[99] Ibid.

[100] Ibid.

[101] Ibid.

[102] Erickson Andrew S and Collins Gabriel. China's Maritime Evolution: Military and Commercial factors. Pacific Focus, Vol XXII, No 2, Fall 2007. pp. 54-55.

[103] Haider Ziad, "Baluchis, Beijing, and Pakistan's Gwadar Port," Georgetown Journal of International Affairs 6, Winter/Spring 2005. pp.95-103.

[104] Ibid.

[105] Ibid.

[106] Stevens Paul. Oil and Gas Pipelines: Prospects and Problems. NBR Special Report 23, Sept 2010. pp. 10-12.

[107] Holmes James. China's Maritime Strategy is More Than Naval Strategy. The Jamestown Foundation. China Brief Volume: 11 Issue 6. 08 April 2011. p.1.

[108] Ibid.

[109] Ibid.

[110] Ibid.

[111] Luttwak Edward. The Political Uses of Sea Power. Johns Hopkins University Press, Baltimore, 1974. pp. 6-11, 39-40.

[112] Holmes James. op cit.

[113] "People's Liberation Navy – History", available at http://www.globalsecurity.org/ military/world/ china/plan-history.htm, accessed on 09 Dec 2010.

[114] United States DoD. loc cit.

[115] Shambaugh David. op cit. p 226.

[116] Muller David G. op cit. pp. 13-40. This comprised a force of nearly 350 warships, submarines and small combatant craft. While many of these were capable of offshore operations, they were kept close to home. Moreover, there was virtually no auxiliary force to sustain offshore operations.

[117] Shambaugh. David. op cit, p. 307.

[118] Muller David G. op.cit. p.51.

[119] Fisher Jr Richard D. loc cit. pp. 123-124,148.

[120] Thapliyal Sheru Maj Gen. PLA's New Mantra- Building Capabilities, AGNI Vol. XII. No III, p. 21. See also United States DoD. Annual Report to Congress, loc. cit, p. 11.

[121] White Paper on China's National Defence in 2008 available at http:// english.gov.cn/official/ 2009 01/ 20/ content_1210227.htm, pp.47,23-24, accessed on 16 Sep 2010.

[122] Cooper Cortez A. The PLA Navy's New Historic Missions. RAND Testimony CT 332, Jun 2009, p. 4, available at http://www.rand.org/pubs/testimonies/CT332/ . Accessed on 09 Sep 2010.

[123] Cole Bernard. China's Naval Modernisation: Cause for Storm Warnings. NDU Symposia 2010. pp. 8-9.

[124] Ibid.

[125] Qi Xu, "Maritime Geostrategy and the Development of the Chinese Navy in the Early Twenty-First Century," Naval War College Review 59, Autumn 2006. pp. 46, 54-55.

[126] Ibid.

[127] Ibid. pp. 56-63.

[128] Ibid.

[129] White Paper on China's National Defence in 2006 available at http:// www.china.org.cn/english/ features/book/194421.htm, accessed on 16 Sep 2010.

[130] White Paper on China's National Defence in 2006 available at http:// www.china.org.cn/e-white/20041227/index.htm, accessed on 16 Sep 2010.

[131] White Paper on China's National Defence in 2010 available at http://www.gov.cn/ english/official/2005-08/17/content_24165.htm#2011, accessed on 16 Jul 2011.

[132] Ibid.

[133] Ibid.

[134] Ibid.

[135] Ibid.

[136] Ibid.

[137] Ibid.

[138] The PLA Navy. op. cit, pp.23-26.

[139] United States DoD 2011. op cit. p. 23.

[140] Qi Xu. op cit. pp 56-57. Chase Micheal S and Erickson Andrew S. The Jamestown Foundation. China Brief Volume: 9 Issue 19. 24 Sept 2009. p.1.

[141] United States DoD 2011. Ibid.

[142] Qi Xu. op cit.

[143] The PLA Navy. op. cit, p. 7.

[144] Ibid.

[145] Ibid.

[146] Ibid.

[147] United States DoD 2011. op cit.

[148] The PLA Navy. op. cit.

[149] Amit Singh. South China Sea Dispute: A New Area of Global Tension. NMF Commentary. pp. 2-3

[150] Ibid.

[151] Ibid.

[152] Ibid.

[153] Ibid.

[154] Pandey Dr. Sheo Nandan. Coping with the Rise of China: Imperatives for South Asia, ISPSW Journal, Jan 2011, p. 6, available at http://www.isn.ethz.ch/isn/Digital-Library/Publications/Detail /?id =125885, accessed on 05 Jan 2011.

[155] Ibid.

[156] Guanglie Liang, Chinese Defence Minister. China Preparing for Conflict in Every Direction, as quoted in Beijing News Net, available at http://www.telegraph.co.uk/news/worldnews/asia/china.html accessed on 29 Dec 2010.

[157] Mote FW. op. cit. pp. 616-617.

[158] Ibid.

[159] Parit Parama Sinha. China's Soft Power in Asia, RSIS Working Paper No 200, 08 Jun 2010, pp. 6-11.

[160] Mishra Brajesh. op cit. p. 6.

[161] Ibid.

[162] Ibid.

[163] Chase Micheal S. op cit.

[164] Ibid.

[165] Ibid.

[166] Ibid.

[167] Ibid.

[168] Ibid.

[169] Ibid.

[170] Ibid.

[171] Cole Bernard D. op cit. pp. 3-10.

[172] Ibid.

[173] Ibid. p. 17.

[174] Ibid.

[175] Ibid.

[176] Ibid. p. 21.

[177] Ibid.

[178] Ibid.

[179] Ibid. p. 7.

[180] Ibid.

[181] Ibid.

[182] Ibid.

[183] Ibid.

[184] United States DoD 2011. op cit.

[185] Ibid.

[186] Ibid.

[187] Katoch PC. China :A Threat or Challenge, CLAWS Journal, Summer 2010, p. 80.

[188] Bisley Nick. op cit. pp. 9-11.

[189] Mishra Brajesh. op cit. p. 4.

[190] Bisley Nick. op cit.

[191] Mishra Brajesh. op cit.

[192] Ibid.

[193] Ibid. p. 5.

[194] Ibid.

[195] Grant Charles. India's Response to China's Rise. Centre for European Reform, Issue Brief, 2010. p. 3.

[196] Ibid.

[197] Ibid.

[198] Ibid.

[199] Ibid. p. 4.

[200] Ibid.

[201] China Analysis Brief. loc cit.

[202] Department of Commerce, Government of India, Export Import Data Bank available at http://commerce.nic.in/eidb/iecnt.aspIbid, accessed on 21 Jul 2011.

[203] Ibid.

[204] Ibid.

[205] Grant Charles. loc cit.

[206] Ministry of External Affairs, Government of India available at http:// www.mea.gov.in/ mystart. php?id =8900, accessed on 21 Jul 2011.

[207] Grant Charles. op cit.

[208] Ibid.

[209] Ibid.

[210] Mishra Brajesh. loc cit.

[211] Grant Charles. loc cit. p. 5.

[212] Dali Yang and Hong Zhao. The Rise of India: China's Perspectives and Responses, available at http://www.daliyang.com/files/ Yang_and_Zhao_The_Rise_of_India-China_s_perspectives_and_reponse. pdf accessed on 09 Dec 2010.

[213] Grant Charles. op cit.

[214] Ibid.

[215] Prabhakar W Lawrence S. Ibid. loc cit. p. 41.

[216] Ibid.

[217] Grant Charles. op cit.

[218] Ibid.

[219] Prabhakar W Lawrence. op. cit. pp. 57-58.

[220] Ibid.

[221] Grant Charles. op cit.

[222] Integrated Headquarters of Ministry of Defence (Navy), Freedom to Use the Seas: India's Maritime Military Strategy, 2007, p. 291.

[223] Ibid. pp. 59-60.

[224] Ibid. pp. 83-88.

[225] Holmes James R. India Looking East. The Diplomat, Flash Points, 20 Sep 2011, available at http://the-diplomat.com/flashpoints-blog/2011/09/20/india-looking-east/ accessed on 20 Sep 2011.

Chapter 6
China's Military Ambitions and Balance of Power

China is fast emerging as a potential power of the future both from economic and military point of view.[1] However, it is under global scrutiny as a result of its impressive and massive development in both these spheres.[2] It has over the past couple of years, been able to quickly and strongly recover from the global recession.[3] However, when compared with other global powers its strategic perspectives are divergent from those stated as its development has been at a faster pace in the past two decades with a perceived status of super power which it desires to achieve in the next two decades.[4] It also considers itself eligible to be accorded the status of a global player in the future world order.[5] In order to evaluate China's military and more specifically maritime ambitions in the global matrix and in particular Asia, it would be in order to compare its existing or perceived power equation with the other Asian giant namely India.

While India accepts the future super power status of China and views it as a serious threat, China does not see India as a worthy strategic adversary or an economic competitor in the near future.[6] As part of fulfilling its aspirations of becoming a world power, China has embarked on the path of augmenting its 'Comprehensive National Power' through political, economic, military, technological and diplomatic means.[7] It has taken steps to maintain peace and tranquillity along her borders, including on those with India. As her national strength increases, the use of coercive diplomacy including the threat to use force cannot be ruled out.[8] To this end China looks at next 15 to 20 years as a 'window of opportunity' to gain comprehensive power, while keeping its 'Regional Competitor', India, indirectly contained through the Sino-Pak nexus, strategic encirclement and postponing border settlements.[9]

China does not appear to take India as a serious rival and underplays its standing by looking down upon its economic problems and inability to take on reforms in all fields. The Chinese are critical of India's democratic process which has lead to a very poor pace of change but agree on the fact that perhaps this provides India a degree of stability which may see it through in an economic crisis where as China may not be able to do so in a similar case. China is keeping a close eye on India's growing political and economic sway especially in the Asian region.[10] It considers strong India a challenge to its natural strategic space which it is endeavouring to carve out for itself not only in the Asian region, but beyond that as well. At present, outwardly, China reflects more concern about Japan, US and Taiwan and asserts that it wants to have peaceful and stable relations with its neighbours. China has till recently held the view that the Kashmir problem is bilateral between India and Pakistan and has never interfered in any Indo-Pak skirmish on this issue. Similarly, China is satisfied with India staying out of Tibet issue and appreciates its efforts to quell the movement within India which supports religious freedom and independence of Tibet.[11]

CRITICAL CAPABILITIES AND BALANCES[12]

A techno-economic-military asymmetry between China and India would have a strategic impact on the entire South Asian and Indian Ocean Region. It would impact South Asian neighbours who would approach the two countries differently as some of them are already doing. With the asymmetry in China's favour, it will enhance China's diplomatic and military leverages against India. Even the US and other major powers are more likely to adjust to China's approach, for instance, more say of China in UN reforms as also create nuclear and missile regimes which work against India. The next 10 to 15 year period is crucial for India to close the expanding gap in asymmetries by building fast on its capabilities.

Military Balance

The perception of India about China is that China is no military threat in the near future but regarding the long term, there is a fair degree of uncertainty. India needs to guard against future power projection by China in the Asian region. There has been growing understanding between India and China in the past decade and relations have shown a positive and encouraging improvement. The territorial dispute has been a major thorn in the relations not to forget the other irritant and a matter of concern, which is the growing Sino-Pak relationship especially on the issue of nuclear technology transfer and off late on Kashmir.[13]

The military power differential between India and China has been steadily aggravating over the past decade. In actual terms, with all outlays in place, the differential stands at around 250 per cent annually in China's favour and should be a serious cause for concern in India.[14] If India aims to achieve some semblance of parity with China by 2025, Indian military capabilities and capacities need to be sufficient not only to dissuade, but also to deter. Creation of huge capacity differentials as is the case at present could, simply put, invite attack or aggression, be it on a limited scale or in all probability confined to a particular sector.

As per Military Balance 2011, China outweighs India in every dimension of military capability at an average ratio of 2.5 to 1. This ratio is roughly the same be it while comparing the PLA Army, Navy, Air Force or be it space or cyber assets. However, the present day nuclear differential is heavily tilted in China's favour.[15]

Ground Forces. The People's Liberation Army (PLA) is the world's largest army with 16 lakh men on active service. It has 45 divisions as compared to India's 28; 8,000 main battle tanks as compared to India's 4,000 and around 18,000 artillery pieces as compared to India's 10,000. These figures do not include the armed police or reserves on either side. By 2025 we could see this rise to 60 divisions with the PLA as compared to 35 with India. Main Battle Tanks (MBTs) could be around 12,000 as compared to India's 5,000. Artillery pieces could number 25,000 with China as compared to 11,000 with India. Another area where China scores directly over India is its rapid reaction forces. China through, both, infrastructure and force development has tremendously enhanced its capability to rapidly move and deploy its forces across the length and breadth of its expanse.[16]

Air Forces. India had a qualitative edge as far as combat aircraft and capabilities were concerned till recently. However, the PLA Air Force

(PLAAF) has seen a qualitative as also a quantitative upgrade in the recent past. This advantage, that India enjoyed, has off late given way to parity and is the most ominous in security terms. China has 1,600 combat capable aircraft as compared to India's 630. These figures could rise to 2,300 and 750 respectively by 2025.[17]

Naval Forces. The PLAN in the past has received heavy funding and priority in modernisation due to the Taiwan centric focus of Chinese operational thinking. China's well-articulated strategies of anti-access and area denial have augured well for themself. These have been able to take on the might of the US Navy in and around the South China Sea as well as within the First Island Chain. China has supposedly acquired and demonstrated its ability to hold large ships including aircraft carriers at risk. This critical capability will continue to accrue her tremendous leverage over India in the long run. As against 15 submarines and 43 surface combatants with India, China has 58 submarines and 180 principal surface combatants. This figure is likely to rise to 18 submarines and 120 surface combatants with India as against 120 submarines and 350 surface combatants with China by 2025.[18]

Space and Cyber Assets. China tested its anti-satellite missile in 2007 and in 2010 carried out an anti-ballistic missile test. India on the other hand is far from acquiring this capability. Presently India has around 30 satellites as against an estimated 120 of China (including 60 military and dual use satellites). This figure is well set to rise to 200 of Chinese as against 60 of India by 2025. The Chinese have outdone their Indian counterparts in cyber warfare. China boasts of around 30,000 full time computer professionals in the services and two hacker or Information Technology (IT) brigades as against a very miniscule similar force in the Indian Armed Forces. Chinese for long have been proponents of asymmetric warfare. Their belief is that "If we cannot match you conventionally, we shall defeat you asymmetrically".[19]

Nuclear Forces. As per current estimates China has some 250 warheads in its inventory as against 50 -75 in India. By 2025 these could rise to around 500 with China and around 100 with India. The Chinese arsenal of ICBMs, Intermediate Range Ballistic Missile (IRBMs) and

Submarine Launched Ballistic Missile (SLBMs) disproportionately outnumber those with India. Unless India ups the ante of its indigenous missile development programme, it will continue to be at a severe disadvantage in this critical balance of military power. China's nuclear deterrent is likely to be a more flexible and survivable nuclear force. While China continues advocating its doctrine of no first use, it has off late given indications to the contrary. Doordarshan (DD) India on 07 Jan 2011, citing internal PLA documents, quoted that the Chinese military would consider launching a pre-emptive strike if the country finds itself faced with a critical situation in a war with another nuclear state. It has also inducted and plans to continue inducting more of road mobile and solid propellant systems along with a battery of submarine launched ballistic missiles as part of a credible sea based deterrent. In comparison India continues to battle with its indigenous missile programme which is plagued by delays and cost overlays. Despite India's perspective plans that have been well drawn out both in terms of capability enhancement and threat perceptions, China's strategic forces will far outnumber those of India in both capability and numbers.[20]

Combat Experience. Combat experience is an area where India clearly outscores over China. Having been into more wars than China both before and after independence, Indian forces have proved their mettle every time they have been pushed into battle. Even the 1962 conflict with China would have been a different story had Indian armed forces not been pushed to war with a very myopic vision and imprudent planning on the part of its higher echelons. The Indian side is also rich in experience in CI/CT operations, a fact recognised even by the US. This advantage, coupled with its more focussed and battle tested joint operations capability, should accrue India rich dividends in any future confrontation with China.

Defence Budget

The International Monetary Fund (IMF), in July 2010, released its first detailed assessment of the Chinese economy in four years. This document, although devoid of interesting details made more news for being made public in the first place. The broad conclusions were that the Yuan was undervalued, economic growth vigorous and property values rising too fast. On the contrary, while India is expected to rise at an estimated 8.5 per cent, India's valuations are on the conservative side, unlike that of China. Thus China leverages another point over India in that it can afford to doctor its growth rates, currency valuations as also manipulate international organisations according to its will and requirement.

China's exact military spending is clouded by its relative lack of transparency, unlike that of India. As a rough estimate China's defence spending[21] is three times that of India's when compared as a percentage of each country's Gross Domestic Product (GDP). Looking at India's defence budgets for the last ten years, while the allocations were far below the Chinese defence budgets, the annual increases have not been less impressive. While India has and in all likelihood will maintain an average of around 2.5 - 3 per cent of its GDP on the defence budget, China has attributed its conservatively estimated defence budget of 9 - 12 per cent of the GDP[22] due to the following:-

(a) Increasing salaries and benefits of servicemen.

(b) Compensating for price hikes such as rise in price of food, building materials, fuel, etc.

(c) Pushing forward its military informationisation and moderately increasing funds for equipment and supporting facilities, so as to raise defence capabilities in conditions of informationisation.

China further justifies, according to its White Paper on defence that the total amount and per service person share of its defence expenditure remain lower than those of some major powers of the world. India has neither been in the past nor will be in the future able to justify its increased military spending, if and when it takes place. However, for the two rising powers the annual defence budgets are grossly asymmetrical. Various models of defence budget allocation for China and India up to 2025[23] are tabulated in the comparative chart as given below:-

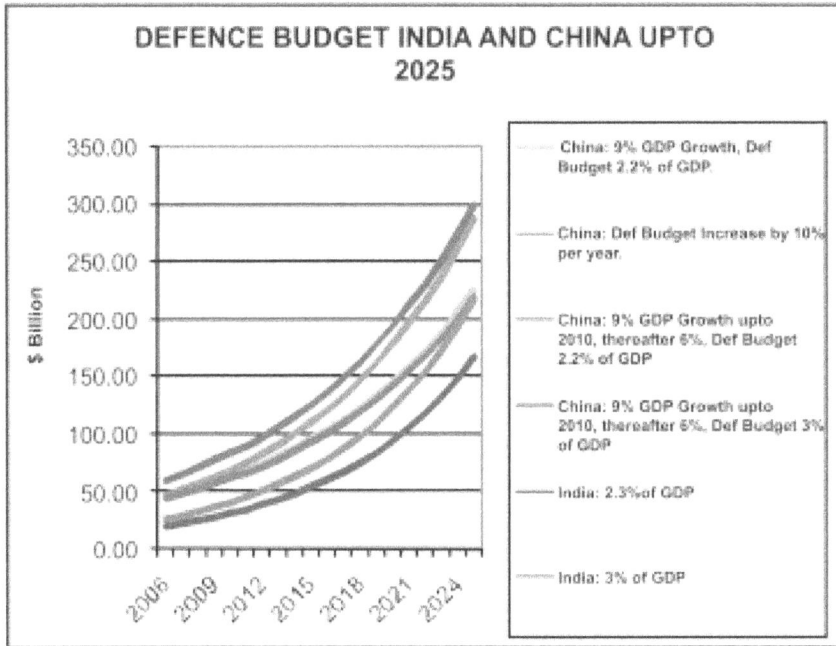

DEFENCE BUDGET INDIA AND CHINA UPTO 2025

Energy Security

On the energy security front, India has lost several rounds of the energy resources game as much to itself as to China over the last few years. In 2009 alone, companies controlled by the Chinese government spent $32 billion acquiring energy and resources assets around the world. In comparison, India's Oil and Natural Gas Corporation (ONGC), also a state-owned company, spent $2.1 billion.[24] From Kazakhstan to Australia, from uranium to natural gas, Chinese state owned companies are grabbing as much of the world's natural resources as they can get their hands on, and reaching for more. On the other hand, the question for India is not how much of the world's resources China ends up controlling, the question is whether India has access to all the resources that it needs.[25]

Despite all these setbacks, India is trying to improve its score. It has set overseas acquisition targets for state-owned corporations and permitted them to spend $1.1 billion without government approval. This might yet produce some results, especially if it is backed by political support. India's strategy must however play to India's strong points while undermining China's advantages.[26] The greatest asymmetries that are in India's favour are democracy and private enterprise. It would be much easier for Indian companies to compete against Chinese ones if the former didn't have the Government of India as the single largest shareholder. In the long term, it is in India's interests for resource rich countries to be democracies. It is also in India's interests to facilitate its private sector to expand globally. Democratic governments are unlikely to necessarily prefer India over China. They are, however, likely to be less susceptible to being bought over.[27]

The current thinking on energy security presumes that the Indian government and by extension, the companies it owns, must be the primary players. This leads to such astoundingly unsound ideas as the Iran-Pakistan-India natural gas pipeline, not only would it place a vital asset in the hands of the Pakistani military-jihadi complex, it involves a risky bilateral commercial deal with the Iranian regime. It is far better to purchase the same gas from Iran as Liquified Natural Gas (LNG), invest in processing terminals all along India's west coast and make it available across India through a system of domestic pipelines. If India invests in LNG infrastructure, Indian energy companies can purchase gas as easily from Russia and Nigeria as from Iran. The government would still have a role, but it would be different. Instead of investing in pipelines, it would need to ensure that the international LNG market is competitive, and secure the world's shipping routes.[28]

Soft Power

The Chinese Communist Party (CCP) is obsessed with building "soft power" as in the attractiveness of China's civilisation, culture, values and political system and as well as ensuring China is respected and admired for its achievements since reforms began in 1978.[29] In contrast, India puts little emphasis on promoting the country's historical, economic, political and cultural credentials to the world. Its appreciation for the value of "cultural diplomacy" is poor, leave alone understanding the importance of selling its strengths and achievements to the world.

Beijing devotes a sheer amount of economic and human resources to shaping its messages and selling its story.[30] China has funded more than 270 Confucius Institutes in 75 countries, teaching Mandarin and the party's version of history to more than 100 million foreigners. Beijing aims to have over

1000 such institutes running by 2025.[31] In contrast, India has a mere 24 cultural centres in 21 countries functioning under its missions abroad. Beijing's diplomatic charm offensive has been in place since the mid 1990s.[32] At present, China has more diplomats than any other country in the world, including America. In China's state dominated society, diplomats are chosen elite and are given extensive language and cultural training.

Beijing dispatches more diplomatic, business and cultural delegations to all corners of Asia than all other Asian countries combined.[33] In contrast, foreigners complain about the aloofness, ineffectiveness and bureaucratic stubbornness of many of India's diplomatic staff. For a country that vies to be an economic giant and with a population of almost 1.2 billion, official Indian delegations are small, infrequent and poorly utilised.

Indian diplomats might protest that China has significantly more resources at its disposal, its economy is three times larger and its state dominated model places more resources into the hands of the party. But the point is about purpose and intent in promoting a country's soft power, an ambition Beijing has in spades. China measures its progress in terms of Comprehensive National Power, which goes beyond the size of its economy and military, and includes other "softer" capabilities such as the reputation of its economic and political system.[34]

China is now the most unequal place in all of Asia in terms of distribution of income, and absolute levels of poverty have increased since 2000.[35] China has far superior infrastructure but India still uses capital 50 per cent more efficiently than China. This is not to deny India has enormous social and economic problems. The argument is about the importance of soft power and taking the foreign reputation of one's country seriously. Beijing is highly skilled at promoting its achievements and concealing its failings from Western eyes. In contrast, India's failings are openly displayed and New Delhi puts little emphasis on promoting the country's recent achievements, which are considerable.[36]

While few countries trust China, the eagerness to help India continue to rise as is demonstrated by the rapid progress made in its strategic and military partnerships with countries such as the US, Japan, South Korea, Singapore, Indonesia, Vietnam and Australia. India will meet little resistance as it is rising within the existing normative order. But New Delhi's lackadaisical approach to promoting Indian leadership, image and achievements is frustrating for the people who realise the country's importance to the region as a democratic leader and a constraint on Chinese ambitions.

Dependence on Resources

As India and China's economies grow, so does their dependence on access to resources, energy supplies and markets. This in turn plays a crucial part in shaping the two giant's strategic behaviour. While China has charted out a clear and concise path for itself both for the near and long term, India lags way behind in this crucial aspect. India's democratic system while being an asset on one side is very negatively counter balanced by its coalition politics on the other. This compulsion at times becomes an obstacle in India's strategic thought and its long term implications.[37]

India and China have also become locked in urgent competition for energy in the Middle East, Africa, Central Asia and Myanmar. This sense of competition has become all the more urgent for India because of the poverty of its domestic supplies of liquid hydrocarbons and its energy intensive requirements for maintaining economic growth from a low base. Some observers assert that India and China have adjusted their competition for energy such that they do not unduly compete in the same markets and inflate prices as has been the case in the past couple of years.[38]

Demographic Dividend

Both India and China account for almost half the world's population. Demographic pressures will continue to increase in the future, creating a structural constraint on China and India's ability to sustain high growth rates. More than a third of their people will transition from the rural to urban areas by 2025.[39] This will in turn create challenges of employment, infrastructure and housing. India will, at its current growth rate, be the most populous country in the world by around 2035.[40] However, one thing that India will clearly score over China is that while India will have a large younger population to harness potential from, China will be burdened by an over aging senior citizens force. This demographic dividend needs to be well exploited by India in order to leverage advantage over China. This should in theory erode China's comparative advantage in labour intensive manufactures by about 2025.[41]

Economic Liberalisation and Trade

In the initial stages of India's economic liberalisation, some experts claimed that India had a leapfrog economy that would bypass the labour intensive phase altogether. Until quite recently, India's labour intensive push into the world markets was restrained not so much by tariff policy as by foreign direct investment restrictions, labour laws, lack of infrastructure and state imposed restrictions on the large scale manufacturing sector, which had the effect of reserving labour intensive manufacturing for the small scale sector. On the other hand, the enormous capitalisation of the Chinese economy also promises to enable it to substitute capital for labour on an immense scale as its labour force ages, ensuring that it retains a formidable competitive edge and a substantial share of the world economy.[42]

The Sino Indian relationship is worryingly ambivalent. On one side of the equation we see a flourishing people to people relationship underwritten by what is projected to be one of the world's largest bilateral trading partnerships sometime between 2010 and 2020. In the past decade trade between the two countries has grown at a phenomenal average.[43] China and India have also made a mutual decision to set aside fighting about their disputed border while the two giants develop their economies and enter world markets, known in the case of China as the 'peaceful development' doctrine.[44]

It is however a matter of concern that India's trade deficit with China has been growing and now stands at more than United States (US) $ 16 billion.[45] As Chinese imports increase into what should be a labour intensive Sino Indian relations and the rise of China manufacturing country, the vaunted trading 'revolution' could look less promising from the Indian perspective. India asserts that China is dumping large quantities of manufactured goods onto the Indian market. New Delhi has refused vital Chinese investment in key areas that it considers to be security risks, such as telecommunications and port development. It continues to deny China market economy status and resists China's offer of a free trade agreement.[46]

Water Issues

Closely associated with border issues is the issue of water. China's plans to divert 40 billion gallons of water annually from rivers in Tibet especially the massive Yalong Tsangpo, which becomes the Brahmaputra in India and subsequently the Megnad in Bangladesh to the arched Yellow River Basin are causing considerable concern in India and Bangladesh. The situation is exacerbated by the melting of the Himalayan glaciers that feed the great rivers of Asia, on which 47 per cent of the world's population depends. If not resolved early and amicably, China will acquire great power leverage over India, resulting in avoidable tensions between the two countries.[47]

China and the Indian Ocean Region

China's growing footprint in the Indian Ocean, and especially in South Asia, is a cause for concern in India as it is surrounded by vulnerable borders and volatile countries with which it is often at loggerheads. China is selling weapons to all of India's immediate neighbours except Bhutan and constructing deep water ports in Myanmar, Bangladesh, Sri Lanka and Pakistan. Although claims of Chinese military bases in Myanmar are exaggerated, India feels surrounded in its own backyard. Given this ambivalent relationship, it is not difficult to imagine that if China continues to surpass and draw away from India economically and strategically, as appears to be the case on present indications, such ambivalence will soon give way to wariness, concern and, ultimately, the more overt desire to balance China's rise.[48]

Infrastructural Capability

The infrastructural differential between China's logistic capacity and capability in Tibet and Xinjiang is far beyond that of India in the Himalayan region. The Qinghai Tibet Railway (QTR) gives China the advantage of moving up to 11 trains on a daily basis into Tibet. By 2025 it plans to extend this railway to Nepal and Chumbi Valley. On the other hand India's railway project in Jammu and Kashmir is moving at a very slow pace. Also the road connectivity in India along the Line of Control / Line of Actual Control (LOC/LAC) although being extended up to the borders is way behind schedule and lacks capacity as well as alternate axis.[49]

Conclusion

It is perceived that besides China's raising the bogey of border dispute from time to time which has not been addressed by India from a position of strength as desired, deliberate arming of Pakistan by China cannot be overlooked forever. Chinese strategy of concirclement of India is a clear strategic threat and not merely an energy security issue. As part of grand strategy towards containment of India in its progress and development, China is supporting Pakistan to keep India preoccupied while she promotes her interest and competes for influence in rest of South Asia.[50]

Endnotes

[1] Prabhakar W Lawrence S. China's Strategic Culture and Current International Dynamics: Perspective From India, The Rise Of China, Pentagon Press and ORF, p. 37.

[2] Liu Xuecheng. China's Strategic Culture and its Political Dynamics. The Rise of China, Pentagon Press, 2008, p. 1.

[3] Mohan Raja C. Power and Paradox: The Future of Sino-Indian Relations, Think India Quarterly, Vol13, No 2, Apr-Jun 2010, p. 207.

[4] Ibid.

[5] Ibid.

[6] Dali Yang and Hong Zhao. The Rise of India: China's Perspectives and Responses, available at http://www.daliyang.com/files/Yang_and_Zhao_The_Rise_of_India-China_s_perspectives_and_ reponse.pdf accessed on 09 Dec 2010.

[7] United States DoD. Annual Report to Congress, "Military Power of the People's Republic of China 2009" , pp. 2-3.

[8] Katoch PC. China :A Threat or Challenge, CLAWS Journal, Summer 2010, p. 80.

[9] Ibid. p. 85.

[10] Prabhakar. op. cit. pp. 57-58.

[11] Li Zhang. China-India Relations: Strategic Engagement and Challenges, Centre for Asian Studies, IFRI, Sep 2010, pp.25-32.

[12] Bakshi GD. The Chinese Threat in Perspective, CLAWS Journal, Summer 2010, p. 57.

[13] Subrahmanyam K. Countering China's New Assertiveness available at http://business-standard.com/ india/storypage.php?autono=406992 accessed on 07 Sep 2010.

[14] Bakshi. op. cit.

[15] The Military Balance 2010. The International Institute for Strategic Studies. pp. 464-465.

[16] The force projection for 2025 is based on inputs from various Chinese and Indian media and internet reports; list of forces, weapons and platforms is as given in Jane's Armed Forces 2011 and The Military Balance 2011 as also an analysis of decommissioning and phasing out of older forces, weapons and platforms. Also see Bakshi. op. cit. p. 59.

[17] Ibid. Bakshi. op. cit. p. 58.

[18] Ibid. Bakshi. op. cit. p. 59.

[19] Ibid.

[20] Ibid. Bakshi. op. cit. p. 58.

[21] United States DoD. Annual Report to Congress, op. cit, p. 32.

[22] White Paper on China's National Defence in 2008 available at http://english.gov.cn/official/ 2009 01/ 20/ content_1210227.htm, p. 47, accessed on 16 Sep 2010.

[23] Ibid. United States DoD. Annual Report to Congress, loc. cit, p. 32. China Economic Forecast to 2040 and Defence Budgets available at http://www.globalsecurity.com/2010/03/china-economic-forecast-to-2040-and.html accessed on 08 Nov 2010.

[24] Katakey Rakteem and Duce John. India Loses to China in Global Race to Secure Energy Assets, available at http://oilandglory.foreignpolicy.com/category/region/south_asia accessed on 07 Sep 2010.

[25] Ibid.

[26] Ibid.

[27] Ibid.

[28] Integrated Headquaters of Ministry of Defence (Nav0), Freedom to Use the Seas: India's Maritime Military Strategy, 2007, pp. 46-49.

[29] Lee John. Will China Fail, Federation Press, 2007, p. 19.

[30] Parit Parama Sinha. China's Soft Power in Asia, RSIS Working Paper No 200, 08 Jun 2010, p. 2.

[31] Ibid, p. 6.

[32] Ibid, pp. 6-8.

[33] Ibid, pp 6-11.

[34] Guanglie Liang, Chinese Defence Minister. China Preparing for Conflict in Every Direction, as quoted in Beijing News Net, available at http://www.telegraph.co.uk/news/worldnews/asia/china.html accessed on 29 Dec 2010.

[35] The 2010 Legatum Prosperity Index Full Report. Legatum Institute, pp. 17-19.

[36] The 2010 Legatum Prosperity Index Brochure. Legatum Institute, pp. 6-15.

[37] Katoch. op. cit, p. 80.

[38] US Energy Information Administration / International Energy Outlook 2010. Highlights, pp. 2-6.

[39] National Intelligence Council. Global Trends 2025: A Transformed World, US ONI, Nov 2008, pp. 8-19.

[40] United Nations. World Population to 2300. Department of Economic and Social Affairs, Population Division, p. 27.

[41] Ibid, p.20.

[42] Ibid, pp. 29-31.

[43] Ibid, p. 30.

[44] Prabhakar. op. cit. p. 41.

[45] Government of India, Ministry of Commerce available at http://commerce.nic.in/eidb/default.asp accessed on 08 Nov 2010.

[46] Siddiqui Huma. The Financial Express: Krishna to take up Growing Trade Defeciet with China, available at http://www.financialexpress.com/news/krishna-to-take-up-growing-trade-deficit-with-china/599870/ accessed on 06 Sep 2010.

[47] IDSA Task Force Report. Water Security for India: The External Dynamics, IDSA, 2010, pp. 67-68.

[48] Katoch. op. cit, pp. 81-82.

[49] Bakshi. op. cit. p.60.

[50] Bakshi. op. cit. pp.55-57.

Chapter 7

The People's Liberation Army Navy in Mid Twenty First Century and Its Role in Global Security-A Prognosis

In war, numbers alone confer no advantage. Do not advance relying on sheer military power.

- Sun Tzu, The Art of War

China's rise over the past few years has drawn a great deal of global attention. Most notably, China's growing economic dynamism has made it a powerful actor in the globalised economy.[1] This continuing growth of China's economy requires secure access to foreign energy resources.[2] In response to this need, the PLAN of the PRC has been undergoing an expansion and force modernisation process that is intended to ensure that China has access to energy resources via well-guarded SLOCs.[3] The overall nature and impact of China's expanding maritime strategy remains unknown as has been brought out in the preceding chapter.

In order to crystal gaze into the future and bring out a prognosis of the PLAN in the mid twenty-first century and its role in global security, it is necessary to study some erstwhile global maritime powers and their rise. In recent history, post-Meiji Restoration Japan and late-nineteenth/early-twentieth century Germany provide two historical examples of the impact of rising economic powers with expansive maritime strategies.[4] A review of both case studies will assist in assessing the potential ramifications of China's expanding maritime strategy for regional and global security.

Provisions of the United Nations Convention on the Law of the Sea (UNCLOS) guarantee the freedom to use the seas. This guarantee ensures open access to energy resources that fuel modern economies, as well as the free exchange of the finished goods those economies create.[5] Toward that end, the United States has developed the most technologically capable navy in the world. Capable of operations worldwide, no other navy challenges the dominance of the United States Navy (USN) on the high seas. However, some analysts see a growing PLAN as a potential threat to the USN's dominance in the Western Pacific and beyond. In order to accurately assess the nature and degree of threat that the PLAN presents not only to the USN, but also the Asia Pacific regional navies, it is necessary to take into account both the reasons behind China's drive to establish a more capable navy and the potential ramifications of a larger PLAN.[6]

The key area of concern for navies worldwide and more specifically for those of the Asia Pacific, is how to respond to the PLAN's increased force structure.[7] Historically, two periods in modern history demonstrate the effects of the expansion of a rising power's naval force structure alongside that of the navy of a geopolitically dominant state – post-Meiji Japan and the Second German Reich. An analysis of the rise of the Imperial Japanese Navy prior to World War II and the rise of the Imperial German Navy prior to World War I will present general themes that occur over the course of significant naval arms expansions.[8]

Along with the economic and political aspects of national power, the military dimension of the rise of the People's Republic of China (PRC) is a topic of great speculation and, more often than not, concern. In particular, the PLAN stands out as a highly dynamic sector of the Chinese military. Current trends indicate that the Chinese naval fleet will surpass the world's largest navy, that of the United States, in number of vessels by 2015.[9] Discernible motivations for China's continued naval modernisation range from the desire to establish PRC domination of Taiwan via military force to the capacity to guard offshore energy and sovereignty issues.[10]

Of key interest to the Asia Pacific states is the fact that, "observers believe that broader goals of China's military modernisation include defending China's claim in maritime territorial disputes and protecting China's SLOCs".

Both maritime territorial disputes and the protection of SLOCs highlight a key consideration for Chinese policy makers in that transport by sea is China's most viable mode of energy supply. In light of that fact, some Chinese strategists have argued for increased funding of the PLAN because "access to the sea is an indispensable condition and decisive factor for China's rise."[11] PLAN modernisation is a direct reflection of the Chinese leadership's awareness that over 80 percent of China's oil imports pass through the Malacca Straits – a chokepoint where the Chinese have no tangible military presence and are unable to guarantee freedom of the seas.[12] The available literature on the PLAN indicates that the PRC is intent on expanding the size and operational sphere of the PLAN. Looking at the causes and effects of previous naval force expansions by regionally rising powers will provide a broader perspective from which the PLAN's expansion and modernisation may be better understood.

Following the Meiji Restoration of 1868, the leaders of Japan inaugurated a concerted program of modernisation and industrialisation that revolutionised the country. A common theme in the literature on the rise of Japan's navy notes that, along with the economic growth of Imperial Japan, "the Imperial Japanese Navy was emblematic of the rise of Japan as a world power."[13] Within decades of embarking on modernisation, Japan had the third largest navy in the world. Literature that outlines why Japan's navy grew so quickly is not as abundant as sources that outline how the Navy grew. However, the available literature agrees that there were both economic and political justifications for the navy's growth.[14]

The Japanese Navy "secured and defended Japan's colonial interests and demonstrated to the world that Japan had emerged as a modern industrial power."[15] Economically, colonial interests provided essential raw material for the Japanese economy, while the international respect garnered from Imperial Japanese Navy's (IJN) defeat of both Chinese and Russian forces around the turn of the twentieth century served Japan's political objective of regional power and influence.[16] The success of Japan's naval expansion had a notable impact on one peer competitor's naval forces. By 1906, the United States Navy had drawn up its official War Plan Orange, a detailed plan of how to counter Japanese aggression in the Western Pacific, which shaped American naval strategy for over thirty years.[17] Overall, the connection between post-Meiji Japan's industrialisation and naval expansion is supported by numerous secondary sources, as is the impact of naval expansion upon one of Japan's peer competitors, the United States.

The rise of the Imperial German Navy at the turn of the twentieth century is well covered by secondary sources. Already a powerful industrial force, Germany made a decision in 1884 to pursue overseas colonies.[18]

Colonies would serve as "markets for goods and sources of raw material." Several sources note that Germany's naval establishment assessed Germany's geographic position as poorly suited for maintaining security of trade via SLOCs.[19]

Although the Royal Navy of Britain provided maritime security worldwide, the rise of the Imperial German Navy is widely viewed as an attempt to "protect German merchant shipping and guarantee unimpeded passage to the oceans".[20] Several sources identify Germany's expansive naval strategy as a key component in the escalation of tensions between Britain and Germany prior to World War I. One source specifically notes that, coupled with Germany's economic might and nationalism, "the growing German navy represented a potential hegemonic threat and a cause for concern over the Reich's intentions."[21] A common question that arises both in geopolitics and in literature is, "how does an existing hegemon manage a rising power?"[22] Although not yet a global power, "China's offshore national security concerns are problems whose resolution will require the ability to prevail in a maritime environment."[23] While the PLAN is now only a regional force, the fact that several sources note its developing orientation towards an "offshore active defense" raises questions regarding how the PLAN intends to interact with the predominant maritime power in the region, the United States Navy as also with other Asia Pacific navies.

The rise of China covers several facets of state power and prestige. Foremost among China's strengths is its economy. Along with its economy, China has cultivated diplomatic relationships with numerous powers in both the developed and developing world. Finally, China's military strength is a topic of considerable speculation for both its current strength and the direction of its developments. The combined economic, diplomatic, and military strength of China reveal the country's considerable power, as well as its likely position of dominance within the Asia Pacific in the near future. China's rise raises several issues regarding its place in the international community. Specifically, as China's political, economic, and military power increases, the way in which other countries respond will define the course of international politics for years to come.

With definable and unsecured geographic and economic interests in the sea and with an understanding of naval warfare as both an extension of "active defense" and a distinct form of warfare with a nature of its own, China's naval strategists needed to develop a maritime strategy that could serve China's unique outlook and needs. There are two concerns that are essential to the success of a strategy. The first is a question of the extent to which a strategy achieves national objectives. The second concern relates to the specific strategic culture from which the strategy is developed. With regard to the second concern, a strategy for the PLAN would have to be acceptable to the PLA and Chinese leadership.[24] The strategy chosen in PLAN's case of "offshore active defense" took advantage of China's unique maritime geography and its limited naval forces.

Liu Huaqing's transformation of the PLAN's overall mission was the key turning point in Chinese naval modernisation. Liu ensured that offshore active defense closely mirrored the PLA's active defense doctrine in design. Specifically, offshore active defense includes the necessity of ensuring coastal defense, mobile warfare at sea and the harassment of an enemy far at sea by guerrilla-type units.[25] Combined, these elements would allow for a defence-in-depth through the utilisation of two island chains as offshore lines of defence.[26] The PLAN's new doctrine leverages China's familiarity with land power by defining the offshore objectives of its maritime strategy through adjacent land masses.[27] Additionally, multiple lines of defense allow for flexibility and a degree of uncertainty regarding where the PLAN will emphasise its strength. As depicted in *Figure 1*, the first island chain includes a line that stretches from the southern approaches of the South China Sea, up through the Ryukyu Islands, and finally to the southern tip of Japan. Included within this line are the Yellow Sea, most of the East China, and the whole of the South China Sea.[28] A second island chain stretches from the Kurile Islands in the North, past the Marianas Islands and Guam, finally down through the Caroline Islands.[29]

The aspect of the offshore active defense that appealed to the PLAN's strategists in the PLA is the delineation of the strategy into phases, the use of phases as objectives is traditionally a practice of land warfare where fixed geographic boundaries serve to delineate a military's goals.[30] While the delineation of island chains serves to guide the PLAN in developing increased levels of operational reach, the ultimate long-term objective of the strategy is to consistently increase the offshore range of the PLAN until China is able to field a blue-water force with a global reach. The flexibility of Liu's strategy serves to both conceal the likely maximum geographical objectives of the PLAN and allow for the expansion of the PLAN's mission beyond the currently defined limits.[31]

In keeping with the three aspects of warfare derived from active defense, guerrilla warfare, mobile warfare, and positional warfare, a PLAN planned around the offshore active defense would seek decisive strength near-shore, the ability to engage another fleet in the seas near China, and the ability to harass an enemy farther out to sea. The strategic depth and defensive advantages of the offshore active defense are in accord with traditional Maoist strategic thought.[32] Along with the offshore active defense, analysts of the PLAN have identified another key element to China's maritime strategy. In line with Mahan's thought that a maritime power must have production, shipping, and colonies for overseas access, Beijing has initiated dedicated efforts to increase its geopolitical influence through a pattern of offshore presence and economic influence. Termed the string of pearls by Western analysts, the strategy involves the diplomatic and economic development of various nodes, or pearls, along China's SLOC that connect China to the Middle East and beyond.[33]

Figure 1: The First and Second Island Chains [34]

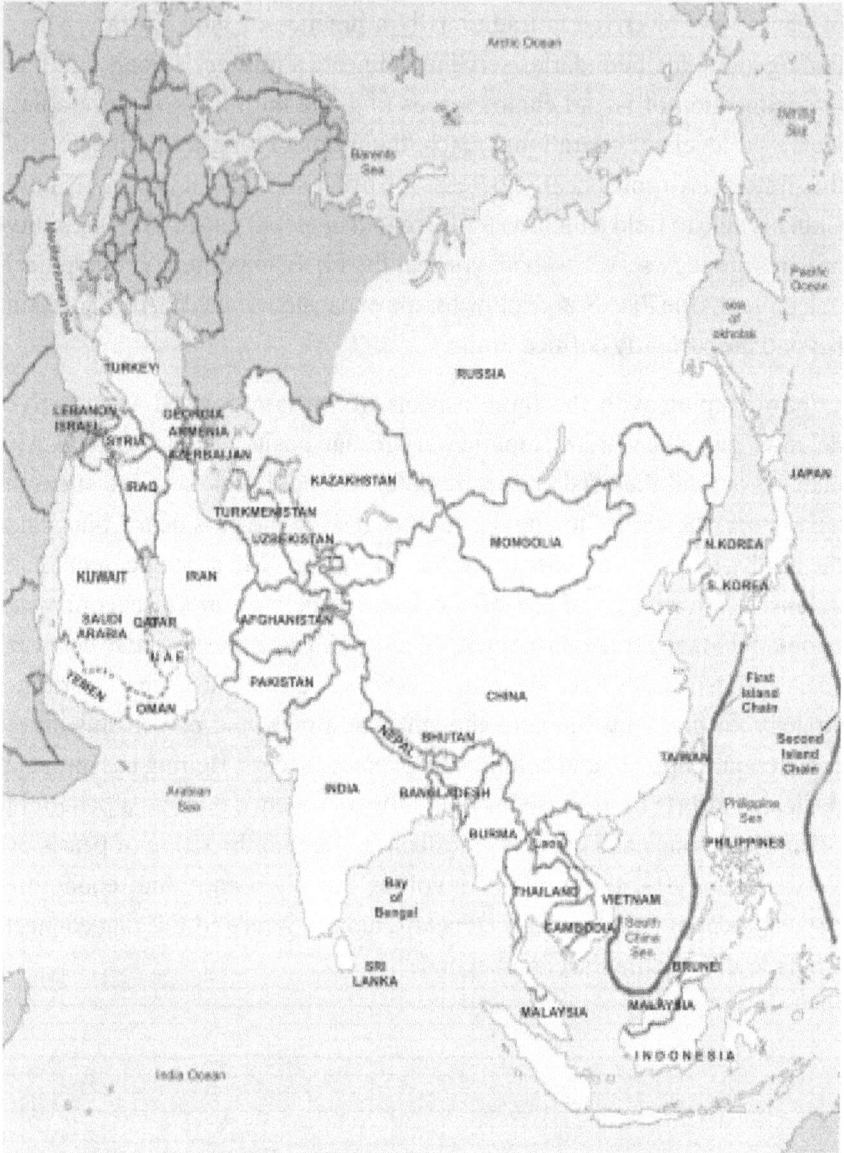

Various measures include investment in the development of deep-water ports at Sittwe and Gwadar, with recent inroads to develop more in the Maldives and Seychelles. Undertaken in an effort to build relationships with countries near China's vital SLOCs, this strategy represents Beijing's attempt to expand not only its military power but also its economic, diplomatic, and ideational power.[35] With 80 percent of its oil imports arriving from Africa or the Middle East, China is developing capabilities specifically to build relationships that will help guarantee China's economic interests in a time of increased competition for natural resources.[36] As China increases its overseas involvement, it comes as no surprise that the PLAN attempts to expand its offshore capability in order to protect China's interests. Beijing recognises the increased importance of overseas development and wishes to ensure its safety; in that light, the argument for a powerful navy, one that does not rely on the goodwill of others to protect China's SLOC and the overseas economic concerns delineated by the capacity building in the Indian Ocean Region and the Asia Pacific, serves as a powerful driving force in an the expansion of the PLAN.[37] Together with the string of pearls strategy of China's foreign policy, the implementation of Liu Huaqing's offshore active defense serves as a powerful driving force in China's maritime strategy. China's maritime strategy has, in turn, served to direct the PLAN's greater force modernisation. A review of the PLAN's force modernisation will highlight both the relative importance of the PLAN in China's defense planning and how well the PLAN's development meets the needs of the broader maritime strategy of China.

The present-day PLAN consists of approximately 268,500 personnel divided equally between officers, non-commissioned officers, and conscripts. With a PLA of 2.3 million, the PLAN makes up 12.6 percent of the total force.[38] Although the PLA as a whole has undergone several force reductions since 1985, the last force reduction in 2003 called for the reduction of 200,000 positions within the PLA. Notably, while the ground forces were reduced by 1.5 percent, the PLAN was increased by 3.8 percent.[39] The restructuring of the PLA that led to the growth within the PLAN was in consonance with the 2004 China's National Defense white paper's explicitly stated goals of optimizing service composition to increase the size of the technical services (PLAN, PLAAF, and rocket forces).[40] In terms of command structure, the fleet commanders are subordinate to the ground unit commanders in charge of the military regions that contain the fleets. Such a subordination to land forces indicates a secondary role for the PLAN even during a time of maritime conflict.[41] The command relationship is further confused by the PLA's distinction between military rank and positional rank. Fleet commanders are the same military rank as military region commanders, but the positional rank of the fleet is one step below the military region.[42] A change has occurred in the policy-planning level of the PLAN. In 2004, the head of the PLAN, Admiral Zhang Dingfa, was added to the body that commands the whole of the PLA, the Central Military Commission.[43] Although Zhang was personally promoted in positional rank, the PLAN as an organisation was not simultaneously elevated in positional status. The PLAN remains subordinate to the ground forces' four general departments, a situation that provides the PLAN with a voice at the highest levels of China's defense policy-makers while still keeping the service subordinate to the institutionally dominant ground forces.[44]

In terms of budget numbers, Western sources have consistently assessed that the PLA's published budget does not represent the actual defense expenditures of China. Failure to account for various personnel costs, the strategic rocket forces, the paramilitary People's Armed Police (PAP), and foreign military sales handled through the foreign affairs bureaucracy account for the discrepancy. China claimed that its 2011 defence budget was $ 91.5 billion, while the US Defense Intelligence Agency (DIA) estimated China's 2011 military related spending to be between $ 90 and $ 130 billion.[45] As a measure of the service's relative importance within the PLA, the PLAN's percentage of the overall budget has increased during past several decades. One estimate holds that between 1950 and 1980 the PLAN received the smallest percentage of the PLA's budget – 18.4 percent.[46]

A key indicator that Beijing is relying more and more on its navy to shoulder the burden of defense has been the increase in the PLAN's budget percentage since 1980; maritime interests are seen as holding an increased level of importance in China's national defense.[47] By 1991, the PLAN's percentage of the PLA's budget had risen to 32.7 percent.[48] If allocation of funding and resources is an indication of relative importance within the defense planning process, recent decades have seen that the PLAN's importance has dramatically increased. Interestingly, the importance of the military within the greater Chinese budget has decreased in recent years. From 1950 to 1980, the PLA's budget averaged 6.35 percent of Beijing's expenditures; by the 1990s, that percentage had dropped to 1.4 percent.[49]

Additionally, while China's economy has averaged almost ten percent growth since 1980, the average increase in the reported annual defense budget between 1996 and 2006 has been 11.8 percent.[50]

The defense budget increase is not significantly greater than China's GDP growth, indicating that increased Chinese defense budgets are due to the fact that an economically prosperous China has more money to spend. Even taking into account US estimates of a budget higher than what Beijing reports presents a fairly even picture of defense allocation. Between 1994 and 2005, Beijing's announced budget averaged 2.0 percent of national GDP, while US estimates of defense spending as a percentage of China's GDP have consistently been near 8.0 percent on the low end and 11.8 percent on the high end.[51] Beijing's defense spending is significant but, as a share of the overall economy over time, it has remained relatively unchanged. In the end, the increased funding for the PLAN represents an internal reorientation of the PLA towards maritime interests. China's defense budget is growing as China's economy grows. It is the manner of allocation that indicates the central place of the PLAN in fulfilling Beijing's long-term policy objectives.

Divided between the North Sea, East Sea, and South Sea Fleets, China's Navy has a substantial number of vessels. As of 2011, it included at least 72 surface combatants, 58 attack submarines, and 50 heavy and medium amphibious vessels.[52]

Even though it was instituted two years after the 1949 founding of the PLAN, the submarine service is listed first in order of protocol among the five branches of the PLAN (submarine forces, surface forces, naval aviation, coastal defense, and Marine Corps).[53] Since 1990, the submarine force has decreased in number from 92 to only 58 hulls. However, the number of high-tech hulls has increased during that same period from one to 22.[54] Among those high-tech hulls, China has recently acquired eight Russian-made Kilo submarines; diesel-powered boats capable of firing modern SS-N-27 Sizzler Anti-Ship Cruise Missiles (ASCMs).[55] The Russian-made submarines join a force of domestically produced hulls that include the high-quality Song and nuclear-powered Shang submarines. Based on the production-rate of higher-end hulls, combined with the acquisition of Russian hulls, foreign analysts have developed a degree of respect for China's industrial and technological capacity to develop a competent and effective submarine force.

The surface forces of the PLAN have also undergone significant modernisation. Since the 1990s, China has purchased four Sovremmeny class destroyers from Russia, each capable of carrying the SS-N-22 Sunburn ASCM.[56] The Sovremmeny class destroyers are complemented by a total of eight new indigenously produced destroyer and frigate classes. Of the destroyers, nine hulls of five different classes have been produced, while 16 frigate hulls of three classes have been produced. Aside from the significant anti-surface capabilities of the Sovremmenys, the general trend in China's surface force is to develop improved anti-air capabilities. The newest destroyer-class, the Luzhou, appears to be built specifically as an anti-air platform. Although only two are in service, the Luzhou-class carries the SA-N-6 surface-to-air missile (SAM), capable of intercept at distances up to 50 nautical miles.[57] Altogether, the Chinese surface force represents an attempt to solidify anti-surface force while developing China's lagging anti-air capability.

A topic of great speculation has been that of China's induction of an aircraft carrier. China's likelihood of early operationalisation and fleet integration of a fully functional carrier will depend on two factors. The first is how well the PLAN's current operational doctrine incorporates a carrier into its design.[58] Within the PLAN, an aircraft carrier is seen as a key symbol of a powerful nation. During an interview regarding the PLAN's aircraft carrier plans, PLAN Senior Colonel Zhang Chengmao was clear as to the value of a carrier for China's fleet: The modern aircraft carrier is a reflection of the great power of a nation's navy. It is also a comprehensive reflection of the political, economic, national defense, and scientific and technological power of a nation. From a certain perspective, possessing a modern aircraft carrier is not only an indication of whether or not a navy is powerful, but is also a reflection of a nation's naval strategy and overall national strength.[59] Unfortunately, while air coverage over the South China Sea would assist the PLAN in controlling it, should the need arise, the current PLA focus on the return of Taiwan does not require the PLAN to field aviation assets far out to sea. Shore-based aircraft are adequate for that task.[60] A carrier's value to China's prestige is thus not matched by China's immediate strategic requirements.

The second issue is cost. China has attempted to acquire carriers through foreign purchase. In the recent past, China has acquired four out-of-service carrier hulls, the former HMAS Melbourne, and ex-Russian ships Minsk, Kiev, and Varyag. With the exception of the Varyag, these vessels have since been either dismantled or turned into tourist attractions. The most likely reason is cost – the cost of refitting an aircraft carrier is prohibitive. Estimates of the Indian Navy's attempt to refurbish the ex-Russian carrier Admiral Gorshkov at a cost of around $ 2.2 billion would be far too taxing to the PLA.[61] With the requirement of three carriers in order to field one at sea (one in work-up, one in overhaul), the total cost of $6.0 billion to refurbish, equip, and man a carrier and carrier air wing, one effective aircraft carrier would require between 5.7 to 8.5 percent of the PLA's budget.[62] China may choose to pursue a helicopter carrier, but a blue-water aircraft carrier capable of dedicated air control is not in accord with either the PLA's most pressing strategic concern, Taiwan, or its budgetary restrictions.

The PLANAF suffers from its secondary status to both the PLAN's submarine and surface forces and the PLAAF. The most important element within the PLANAF is its helicopter force. The first Chinese service to use helicopters, the PLANAF continues to provide support to surface vessels at sea. Unfortunately, the PLANAF lacks critical fixed-wing capabilities, including antisubmarine warfare (ASW) platforms and a lack of effective in-flight tankers.[63] While the shore-based bomber fleet is outdated, modernisation to the PLAN's fighter component has been extensive.

A key aspect of China's naval strategy is its missile inventory. Advanced ASCMs like the SS-N-22, Sunburn, and SS-N-27, Sizzler, have been acquired and Surface-to-Air (SAM) Missile systems have been improved to cover the whole of the Taiwan Strait. Of more pressing concern is the large numbers of Short-Range Ballistic Missiles (SRBMs) China has acquired. As of December 2010, the US Department of Defense (DOD) estimated that between 1,000-1,200 SRBMs, particularly CSS-6 and CSS-7 missiles capable of hitting targets up to 350 nautical miles from shore, are aligned across from Taiwan; estimates are that number will increase by 100 missiles per year.[64] Of particular note, the PLAN has reportedly developed the ability to attack vessels at sea using SRBMs equipped with maneuvering re-entry warheads.[65] Designed particularly for use against approaching aircraft carriers, these carrier-killing SRBMs launched from shore indicate a near-shore anti-access intent, one that fits well with China's desire to keep other forces, notably the US, from interfering with a theoretical military action against Taiwan.

Reviewed as a whole, the Chinese fleet modernisation appears directed towards denying access to interlopers near China's shore. This particularly suits the desire to prevent interference in case of a conflict with Taiwan. Increased anti-air capability on surface platforms would help deny air superiority to opponents when those platforms sail to the South China Sea. Otherwise, the emphasis on submarines and missile systems, both shore and sea based, that would slow an intruder are in line with the active defense precept of utilising the ocean as a defensive barrier against attack. China is slowly developing forces that can move farther from shore, but the still limited capability to logistically support these forces indicates that command-of-the-sea along China's SLOCs is still a goal for the PLAN. At best, sea-denial is the doctrine with which China is most capable of achieving proficiency.

With an economy that requires guaranteed access to offshore energy resources coupled with significant sovereignty issues, China will determine the worth of the PLAN by its ability to deter external interference in what Beijing considers internal territorial matters. Additionally, as oil is Beijing's most prominent offshore economic interest,[66] the PLAN's capacity to secure vital sea lanes over which resources are transported is a defining task in the PLAN's modernisation. With territorial claims that lie beyond the accepted norm of international law and a rapaciously hungry economy, Beijing has presented its navy with a significant challenge. Although China's military has a traditionally continental orientation, the PLAN has successfully utilised Mao's active defense to define a strategy at sea that both serves to define China's maritime boundary and provides a justifying narrative for increased allocation of resources to the PLAN.

The United States presents the perfect antagonist within the active defense paradigm. As China is the weaker power, a short term goal that directs the PLAN's modernisation is the ability to threaten US naval power, particularly aircraft carriers, with a strategic defense centered on submarine and surface forces. The PLAN's modernisation in these areas directly reflects Beijing's desire for the PLAN to act as an anti-access force.[67] In the longer-term, the very forces used to prevent interference near shore, and particularly in the case of a conflict with Taiwan, will have the capacity to sortie further from shore in order to protect SLOCs and distant maritime resource interests.[68] The increase in PLAN's Anti-Air-Warfare (AAW) capability would permit a task force to deny an opposing land-based or maritime force the ability to freely challenge Chinese movement in distant regions with air power. Developments in the PLAN's surface and submarine forces clearly indicate that Beijing is planning to leverage its naval force to prevent others from interfering with China's broader maritime strategy of sea lane security and maritime resource development.

True command-of-the-sea is both difficult and too costly for Beijing to contemplate. While an aircraft carrier capability would increase China's assessment of its comprehensive national power, the use of non-military tools within China's string of pearls compensates by involving China directly in the maritime interests of other nations. Militarily, China has decidedly chosen to focus its PLAN modernisation around the principle of sea denial.[69] The 2004 China's National Defense white paper indicates that the more defensively oriented sea denial is a conscious choice within Beijing's leadership: The PLA Navy is responsible for safeguarding China's maritime security and maintaining the sovereignty of its territorial seas along with its maritime rights and interests. The Navy has expanded the space and extended the depth for offshore defensive operations.[70]

While partly influenced by China's traditionally defensive rhetoric, the idea of offshore defensive operations as an objective of the PLAN is matched by Beijing's recent focus on submarine and near-shore defensive forces. Unable to challenge the predominant naval power of the time, the USN, the PLAN is ably developing its capacity to challenge the USN's absolute freedom of movement at sea. To a degree, China is adjusting well to its inferior status. As Corbett notes: Where a Power was so inferior in naval force that it could scarcely count even on disputing command by fleet operations, there remained a hope of reducing the relative inferiority by putting part of the enemy's force out of action.[71]

A modern fleet built around the principle of sea-denial represents China's hope of reducing the inferiority of the PLAN when compared to the other navies of the Asia Pacific. With geographically defined strategic depth in the strategy of offshore active defense and a modern fleet of submarines and anti-access surface and missile forces, Beijing is building a force structure that will better allow China to delineate and enforce its maritime economic and sovereignty claims in the East and South China Seas. In time, the extension of maritime power along China's vital SLOCs will increase as the PLAN slowly develops its blue water capabilities.

Chinese security theorists are adamant that, in an age still dominated by great power politics, it is necessary for China to strive to develop a powerful fleet. In Beijing's eyes, China's economic growth is too important to rely upon international cooperation for the movement of resources. Chinese national security expert Ni Lexiong states: Those who believe we don't need a strong navy because international cooperation is the only choice we have to guarantee our life line at sea are misguided in imagining a false premise, i.e., the world has irreversibly been marching toward an eternal peace. This is to use wishful thinking to replace uncertainty. China's considerations for sea power strategy should not be based upon our wishful thinking, but on a realistically established sense of uncertainty. Based upon this understanding of our future's uncertainty, it is China's necessary choice to build up a strong sea power we can now conclude that China must establish a strong Navy.[72]

To assess likely effects of China's naval growth and its role in global security, a review of two historical case studies may shed light on general themes that occur when a dominant naval power is challenged by the expansion of a competitor nation's fleet. Both pre-World War II Japan and pre-World War I Germany present two examples of growing economic powers that chose to expand a navy in order to guarantee various offshore interests. By reviewing the actions of both powers, as well as the reactions of their competitors, the United Kingdom and United States, general themes involved in naval arms races may present the United States with options in responding to the growth of the PLAN.

Both Imperial Japan and Imperial Germany were growing powers with maritime ambitions that caused an increase in regional security tensions. The security tensions ultimately led to war. To fully understand the relevance of the experiences of Imperial Japan and Imperial Germany, it is important to analyze broad themes that occur when maritime ambitions challenge dominant powers.

The first theme outlined by the historical case studies addresses signaling. For Japan, a powerful navy was intended to support the ambitions of Tokyo's ever expanding economic sphere of control. From Washington's perspective, the fleet ratios agreed to at both the Washington and London Naval Conferences provided for a fleet size adequate for Japan's needs. To the United States and United Kingdom, why Tokyo demanded a fleet as powerful as the USN and Royal Navy when Japan did not have the geopolitical requirements for such a fleet was in part a mystery. When Tokyo responded to Washington's funding of a fleet that simply met previous treaty agreements with the Second Supplemental building program, the United States felt it had no option but to respond to Japan's threat with its own increased building program. By walking out of the Second London Naval Conference and refusing to engage in further international arms limitations regimes, Tokyo confirmed that it desired a navy as powerful as it could afford. President Roosevelt found it easier to justify a larger USN when Japan acted without fully explaining its naval growth, particularly against a background of what appeared to be unrestrained expansion in China.[73] The failure of Tokyo to signal why it wanted a larger fleet contributed to the unsettled response of Washington and the naval arms race between Japan and the United States.

For Germany, both the commission and omission of poor signals served to upset Great Britain. With the 1898 and 1900 German Navy Laws, London assessed that Berlin was attempting to challenge the Royal Navy's supremacy on the high seas. Berlin's claim to simply want its "place in the sun," an explanation for naval growth that centered on the need to protect imperial ambitions, was unsatisfactory to the Royal Navy. With the passage of the 1906 German Navy Law, a law that directly responded to the Royal Navy's own increased funding and growth, London was certain that Germany's naval growth was intended as a challenge.[74] Unclear early signaling had unsettled the British. The 1906 bill passed by Berlin seemed to confirm the danger that London perceived. With little recourse but to assume that Germany wanted to threaten Britain on the high seas, London enacted larger and larger building programs to ensure the Royal Navy's relative position of superiority over the Imperial German Navy. London had little diplomatic recourse to Germany's efforts without Germany's full disclosure; therefore, a military response to Germany's military actions was the necessary step.

With both Germany and Japan, the perceived need to guarantee economic interests against foreign interference played a significant part in the drive to seek naval strength. Germany's assessment that imported resources were strategically vulnerable and that overseas markets in the form of colonies needed to be secured directly informed Berlin's assessment that a powerful navy had to be formed to protect Germany's interests.[75] Economic insecurity directly informed Berlin's decision to embark on naval expansion. For Japan, the perception within Tokyo was even starker: Japan needed economic autarky.[76] Unable to conceive of engaging in future conflict without first securing economic independence from the interference of others, Japan embarked upon attempts to impose political control over Manchuria, China, and the greater East Asian community.[77] By 1941, unable to guarantee its economic independence after ten years of expansion, Japan was vulnerable to the resource embargoes imposed by the United States. The tensions that led to the embargoes, embargoes brought about because of Japan's continued advance towards political control of East Asian nations, soon led to Pearl Harbor and World War II.

In both cases, attempts to secure economic independence were key factors that pushed each country to seek a more powerful fleet. As economic strength is a key sign of a nation's greatness, the attempts to secure economic independence directly fed another common theme of rising maritime powers – the drive for prestige.

Both Japan and Germany used national greatness as a reason for developing modern battle fleets. In Japan's case, the forced opening of its shores by foreigners who arrived from the sea served as a key motivating factor in ensuring that Japan was a dominant regional naval force. The ratios agreed to under the Washington Naval Treaty system were eventually interpreted by Tokyo as indications of the West's continued lack of respect for Japan.[78] National pride demanded that Japan be treated on equal terms with any Western power; if that could not be agreed upon, military leaders in Tokyo made certain that Japan would not interact in international diplomatic and arms control regimes. Another powerful conclusion that led to naval growth was the assumption that a powerful navy was needed to guarantee the safety of the Greater East Asian Co-Prosperity Sphere, in many ways an ideological construction in which economic anxiety and imperialist arrogance were combined into a single neat package.

Germany's own national pride was directly related to the need to ensure both economic growth and social stability. The imperial turn to Weltpolitik, or world policy, served to direct the competing political energies of the newly unified Germany outward toward a larger world, and away from an increasingly obsolescent authoritarian regime. The conclusion that external sources could serve to both feed Germany's resource requirements while serving as markets for excess industrial goods underlay Berlin's imperial ambitions. Viewing Germany's place amongst the Great Powers of Europe as hindered by a lack of colonies, the German "place in the Sun" ideology, a drive for a worldwide maritime empire, acted as a powerful motivating force in the passage of the German Navy Laws.[79] Defined by its economic needs, Germany's desire for international prestige, a prestige that could be demonstrated with a robust economy and powerful navy, was a key factor in sparking the Anglo-German naval race.

Perhaps the most important theme in both case studies is the futility of a nation-state with a smaller economic and industrial base attempting to match the naval growth of a dominant power. Both Japan and Germany assessed that they would be able to produce enough naval strength if not to defeat outright, then at least to deter, powers which they knew to be stronger on the high seas. As previously outlined, the expectations of Japan and Germany were based on static assessments of their respective peer's industrial capacity. When those peers, the United States and United Kingdom, respectively, responded to the perceived growing naval threat, Japan and Germany were committed to expensive arms races that neither nation could afford. Navies are capital intensive institutions, and they are also wasting assets. Both their operating and their replacement costs must be included in any estimate of their long-term strategic value. The financial calculus of naval power is extremely complex, and for that reason, if for no other, it is better to err on the conservative side. The relative ease with which Great Britain and the United States were able to match and exceed the naval expansions of their rivals caught both Germany and Japan by surprise, and is a clear reflection of the strategic misconceptions, not to say illusions, that underlay their respective building programs.

As history never exactly repeats itself, it is important to understand the similarities and differences of modern China compared to the case studies of Imperial Japan and Imperial Germany. A review of modern China's naval expansion demonstrates several themes in common with the rise of both Japan and Germany. Signaling, economic self-interest, and the ideology of prestige are central factors that indicate China's rise will increase regional tensions.

The PLA budget is an excellent example of poor signaling. Decided upon in secret, it omits key items, which allows China to present an understated image of China's defense growth. The secrecy of the budget may in part be due to China's traditional affinity for deception, but it also reflects its distrust of American motives in Asia. Beijing often assesses Washington's actions in the region as hostile to China's strategic concerns.[80] Additionally, pronouncements from Beijing in recent years have highlighted China's assessment that the risk of global war has been reduced, while the danger from hegemonism and unilateralism, euphemisms for the policies of the United States, are on the rise.[81] Beijing's reluctance to more fully disclose policies, budgets, and objectives obscure the motives behind the growth of the PLAN, particularly its submarine force, which must accordingly be inferred from the identifiable facts at hand, and the explicit pronouncements of the government. Under the circumstances the USN has been inclined to assume that it is facing a severe long-range threat from China, anxieties that are the more credible because the Chinese persistently seem to forgo obvious means of allaying them.

Beijing's economic expansion has prompted it to consider how to secure access to overseas resources; much like Germany and Japan, Chinese scholars have argued for a powerful navy in these terms.[82] Fearing that the

United States might threaten its economy by attacking its energy sources has led Chinese companies to interact with governments that the international community shuns.[83] Iran, Sudan, North Korea, Pakistan and Angola are some of the countries China now assists, to the consternation of the United States and European Union. These commercial efforts provide part of the context within which the world must inevitably view its naval modernisation efforts, which apparently aim to extend China's military reach into the South China Sea and eventually beyond.

The humiliation felt by Japan at the hands of Western Powers was first felt by China. China's capitulation during the Opium Wars was used as an example by the US envoy to warn Japan of the dangers of angering Western powers. Once the most vibrant civilisation on earth, China's desire to return to its status as a great power is a central part of Beijing's present security agenda.[84] One reason that Taiwan figures so high within Beijing's strategic calculus is that recovering the island represents the symbolic ending of China's "century of humiliation."[85] As China drives to overcome decades of humiliation at the hands of the West, the development of a strong navy is seen as a central component expressing China's rightful and natural greatness.

Key differences between China's current situation and the historical cases of Imperial Japan and the Second Reich include the structure of the modern global economy, the ideational shift away from belief in China's cultural dominance, and the size of the PLAN's expansion. These differences, which are specific to China's situation, present mitigating factors that may alleviate rising regional security tensions.

Modern China differs from Imperial Japan in an important way; China is not seeking economic autarky. Although securing energy resources is a central concern for Beijing, China is not nearly as dependent on foreign energy resources as Japan. Japan's military expansion was in part due to its extreme reliance on overseas resource access; barring faith in the market, force would have to guarantee access. While overseas resource access is important to Beijing, it is not a matter of national survival.[86] Therefore, Beijing's desire to build a navy to secure resource access is not as pressing as the need of Imperial Japan.

Compared to Imperial Germany, modern China shares the need to utilise export markets to sell excess manufactured goods. However, China has little need of colonies to ensure export sales; and such arrangements would not be tolerated by the current global system in any case. Instead, modern China has worked diligently to integrate itself into the international economic system. Any impetus on the part of Beijing to strive for economic autarky would be blunted by the very nature of what has enabled China's economic growth – the sale of export goods within the globalised free market system. China needs other countries for its own benefit. As former Chinese leader Deng Xiaopeng noted, "No country can now develop by closing its door. Isolation landed China in poverty backwardness, and ignorance."[87] Under current conditions, autarky is virtually synonymous with under-development.

It is important to note the most pertinent distinction that exists between modern China and the historical case studies – the military budget. The naval arms races initiated by the funding of ship construction by Germany and Japan represented distinct breaks from historic spending levels. As previously outlined, Chinese defense spending has not notably increased as a percentage of overall government spending, or as a share of total national wealth. Using Defence Intelligence Agency (DIA) estimates of the PLA's budget and estimating that the PLAN receives one-third of the PLA's budget, the PLAN's 2011 defence budget equaled between $ 30 to $ 48 billion. When compared to the USN's 2011 budget of $ 160.3 billion, the PLAN simply cannot compete with the USN for fleet funding. The 12.7 percent increase of the 2011 PLA budget over the year before, while higher than normal, provides little cause for concern.

Even a doubling of China's budget would not equate to a navy on par with the USN, unless it was persisted in for decades, during which the United States would of course have ample opportunity to respond. Instead, China's blue-water ambitions have been focused on foreign ship purchases and the development of destroyers and frigates that are providing China with a rudimentary offshore capability. China has focused its naval spending on submarines for a specific reason; submarines best serve an inferior power. Unlike Imperial Japan and Imperial Germany, China recognises that it is the less capable power and apparently does not aspire to challenge the naval superiority of the regionally dominant power – the United States. As it is unable to afford a fleet that could challenge the USN, Beijing has prudently chosen not to try to build a fleet to challenge the USN.

Overall, an analysis of the growth of the Imperial Japanese Navy and the Imperial German Navy provide several broad themes that lend insight into the growth of the PLAN. While China's current naval building is of little immediate concern, Beijing's lack of disclosure to account for the motivation behind its military growth raises questions regarding Beijing's strategic intent. Finally, although certain policy-makers and analysts within Beijing have expressed concern over China's economic dependence on foreign resources and markets, China's current integration into world markets serves to mitigate any attempts to move towards autarky. Contemporary China does not present the same type of threat to the United States that Japan and Germany presented to the hegemonic powers of their day.

China wishes to return to great power status. Implicit in that desire is Beijing's dissatisfaction with the current unipolar system in which the United States is the dominant power.[88] Nevertheless, the naval modernisation of the PLAN is a solid indicator that Beijing's desire to transform the East Asian region into a multipolar region is not a driving force in Beijing's foreign policy. Beijing's current funding for the PLAN is not enough to challenge the strength of the USN where international power interacts most freely at sea. Instead of a strong emphasis on replacing what Beijing perceives as the regional hegemon, Beijing is highly focused on continuing economic development in order to maintain social cohesion and the rule of the Chinese Communist Party.[89]

Another important tool in maintaining China's social cohesion has to do with sovereignty. In the service of sovereignty, China has developed its military to address its most pressing strategic issue – Taiwan. The PLAN has specifically been developed around the problem of Taiwan. Although active defense presents a doctrine that outlines how China can extend its maritime geographic reach, the naval forces Beijing has developed to date are unable to fulfill the requirements of controlling the seas out to the first and second island chains. Instead, near-shore defense and offshore harassment are the hallmarks of a Chinese navy designed around submarines, shore-based fighter and bomber aircraft, and a limited blue-water capability.

The role of the PLAN in Asia Pacific security is one that serves to warn regional and extra regional powers away from China's coast. In China's eyes, that coast includes Taiwan. While outclassed by the USN, the PLAN hopes its sea-denial forces would either threaten or inflict enough damage on any force approaching China that the force would turn away.[90] Although China's long-term interests are to secure its SLOCs and offshore claims, for the foreseeable future, the PLAN will not be able to fully enforce those interests. Instead, China will continue to rely on its diplomatic and economic efforts, efforts such as the string of pearls, while simultaneously building bilateral relationships to ensure that sea-lanes are secured.[91]

Due to the PLAN's historically limited development and China's assessment of the USN's carrier-based maritime dominance, recent growth of the PLAN has focused primarily on the development of an anti-access and area denial forces.[92] China recognises that the PLAN's ambitions should focus on a limited force of high quality that is capable of winning technologically advanced and limited wars at sea.[93] A modern submarine force supplemented with A2AD capabilities is the ideal means by which the PLAN can meet its objective. Such a force is intended to deter the USN's movement near China's coast, most notably in the case of a Taiwan crisis.

Conclusion

Maritime security concerns justify China's development of a modern PLAN that protects China's national interests.[94] China's foremost emerging maritime security concern is the free movement of energy resources via vital SLOCs. To Beijing's disappointment, China's naval modernisation does not fully ensure its maritime interests. To date, the PLAN's growth cannot fully guarantee the security of China's extensive and growing trade and resource requirements. Whatever China's attempts to improve its navy, in the near-term, Beijing must rely on its developing influence via diplomatic and economic efforts such as the string of pearls policy to increase its Comprehensive National Power (CNP). In conjunction with non-military means of guaranteeing sea trade, China must continue to rely upon the United States to militarily secure the vital sea lanes that feed China's ravenous economy.[95] As navy budgets increase with improved technology, the unchanged responsibilities of maritime security must rely more and more upon multinational maritime strategies.[96] The growth of navies has historically indicated a turn towards conflict. Thus China and other Asia Pacific maritime powers have a unique opportunity to identify shared maritime concerns in order to diffuse conflict before it commences.

China is investing in the PLAN for one straightforward reason that, without a capable Navy, it has serious strategic vulnerabilities otherwise not addressable especially in the case of Taiwan. Without a credible naval establishment, it can threaten Taiwan with punishment but not seizure.[97] Given that the strategic case for Navy building emerged some 20 years ago, the CMC and PLA had to choose what sort of Navy to build. The choices were relatively clear. One was the historical model of the IJN. The IJN is tangible proof that a Western-style blue water Navy was possible in an Asian context. But developing such a Navy would have meant a departure from China's continentalist strategic tradition. Besides being countercultural to an Army-dominated PLA, such a blue water Navy would have been expensive and very difficult to make credible in terms of training and technology. China's only attempt to field such a Navy met with disaster in 1895.[98]

The PRC's early relationship with the Soviets provided the second, more obvious, template for the PLA.[99] The geostrategic circumstances facing the Soviet Union and China were similar when it came to threats from the sea, and the defensive Soviet-style anti-access model was also less expensive and easier to build because the PLA could capitalise on Soviet developed technology and operational concepts. Finally, this approach to Navy building fitted within the continentalist worldview at the highest levels of military and party decision making. This approach to Navy building also fits well with the political message that Beijing has been sending to the world: China's rise will be peaceful and nonthreatening.[100] Fielding an obviously defense oriented Navy would be tangible evidence that the PRC was not going to become an expeditionary or power projection threat. Exceptions to this assessment of the PRC as nonthreatening are the cases of Japan and both Koreas. They are within or adjacent to the PLAN sea denial area, the first island chain.

The PLAN submarine force in particular is a capability-based threat to Asia's economic lifelines of maritime trade that the world at large cannot, and probably will not, ignore.[101] For the rest of the Asia Pacific, an avowedly power projection of the PLAN would be counterproductive to China's broader strategic objectives of not creating powerful enemies in the region, especially since such a naval force would not be essential to satisfying the PRC's strategic objectives. In this context, the PLAN's focus on commissioning many more diesel submarines than nuclear submarines could also help reinforce the positive diplomatic message of a peaceful rise. They are quieter, are very hard to find, and create the image of being defensive in nature. They fit within the template of Asia Pacific naval developments that feature South Korea, Singapore, and Malaysia joining Japan, Taiwan, and Australia as nations with conventionally-powered submarines.[102]

It is unlikely that when Liu Huaqing developed his "island chain" approach to maritime strategy, he foresaw the tremendous growth in China's global trade and quest for natural resources especially energy. Nor is it likely that he foresaw the PRC's growing international role in UN peacekeeping. The idea that thousands of PRC citizens would be working or traveling abroad did not seem likely to any student of China twenty years ago. A combination of such factors, plus the pressure from the US and other world powers to become a responsible stakeholder, is creating demand signals for a PLAN that can support UN-sanctioned missions, protect PRC interests abroad with a show of force, protect or evacuate PRC citizens in jeopardy, protect sea lines of communication, respond to natural disasters, and demonstrate the PRC's resolve in support of embattled friends in Africa and along the South Asia littoral. But today these are issues that the PLAN is just beginning to think about seriously. It is not enough simply to think about wartime employment concepts, the PLAN, unique among all of the PRC's military services, would consider distant, prolonged peacetime operations as part of its core mission set.[103]

These combinations of potential missions will require the PLAN to learn how to deploy and sustain surface combatants, amphibious ships, and support ships on distant stations for long periods of time. Also, it will almost certainly create a sound rationale for having a carrier battle group, since helicopters are particularly valued in most of these missions. This means that the PLAN probably faces another addition to its core mission in its future.[104] It will continue to maintain a defensive strategy for the defense of China and its possessions, but it will also deploy a force whose primary utility will be to provide peacetime presence, sea lane monitoring and crisis response.[105] This next-generation Navy will be useful to the PRC in furthering its own interests while also demonstrating that it too can be a responsible stakeholder among military forces of the community of nations.[106]

Endnotes

[1] United Nations. World Population to 2300. Department of Economic and Social Affairs, Population Division, pp. 29-31.

[2] Katakey Rakteem and Duce John. India Loses to China in Global Race to Secure Energy Assets, available at http://oilandglory.foreignpolicy.com/category/region/south_asia accessed on 07 Sep 2010.

[3] United States DoD. Annual Report to Congress, Military and Security Developments Involving the People's Republic of China 2011. p. 21.

[4] Tritle Mathew C. The Growth of PLAN: Impacts and Implications of Regional Naval Expansion. NGS, California, 2007. p.v.

[5] UNCLOS. The States/ Parties to this Agreement, recognize the important contribution of the United Nations Convention on the Law of the Sea of 10 December 1982 to the maintenance of peace, justice and progress for all peoples of the world, while reaffirming that the seabed and ocean floor and subsoil thereof, beyond the limits of national jurisdiction, as well as the resources of the Area, are the common heritage of mankind, while being mindful of the importance of the Convention for the protection and preservation of the marine environment and of the growing concern for the global environment.

[6] Tritle. Ibid, p.1.

[7] Grant Charles. India's Response to China's Rise. Centre for European Reform, Issue Brief, 2010. p. 3.

[8] Tritle. op cit.

[9] O'Rourke Ronald, China Naval Modernization: Implications for US Navy Capabilities – Background and Issues for Congress. Washington, DC: Congressional Research Service, 26 August 2011, pp, 36-38.

[10] Cole Bernard. China's Naval Modernisation: Cause for Storm Warnings. NDU Symposia 2010. pp.3-10.

[11] Christopher Pehrson J, String of Pearls: Meeting the Challenge of China's Rising Power Across the Asian Littoral, US Army War College, Strategic Studies Institute, 2006, p.7.

[12] United States DoD. op cit. p.20.

[13] Bergamini David. Japan's Imperial Conspiracy, Heinemann, London, 1971. Pp. 386-389. David C Evans and Mark R. Peattie, Kaigun: Strategy, Tactics, and Technology in the Imperial Japanese Navy, 1887-1941, Naval Institute Press, Annapolis, 1997. p. xx.

[14] Ibid.

[15] Schencking Charles J, Making Waves: Politics, Propaganda, and the Emergence of the Imperial Japanese Navy, 1868-1922, Stanford University Press, 2005. p, 223.

[16] Bergamini David, op cit.

[17] Sadao Asada, From Mahan to Pearl Harbour: The Imperial Japanese Navy and the United States, Naval Institute Press, Annapolis, 2006. p, 23.

[18] Massie Robert K, Dreadnought: Britain, Germany and the Coming of the Great War, Ballantine Books, New York, 1991. p, 85.

[19] Hobson Rolf, Imperialism at Sea: Naval Strategic Thought, the Ideology of Sea Power and the Tirpitz Plan, 1875-1914, Brill Academic Publishers, Boston, 2002. pp, 123-125. Holmes James R. Mahan, a Place in the Sun and Germany's Quest for Sea Power. Comparative Strategy, 2004. pp, 23, 45-46.

[20] Massie. Ibid, p, xxiv.

[21] Hobson. Ibid, p, 326.

[22] Mishra Brajesh. Keynote Address, China's Quest for Global Dominance: Reality or Myth. Ed Sandhu Maj Gen PJS. Vij Books, New Delhi. p. 4. Yoshihara Toshi and Holmes James, Command of the Sea with Chinese Characteristics. Orbis 49, 2005. p, 691.

[23] Cole Bernard, The Great Wall at Sea: China's Navy Enters the 21st Century. Naval Institute Press, Annapolis, 2001. p, 9.

[24] Barnett Roger W, Strategic Culture and it Relationship to Naval Strategy, Naval War College Review 60, No 1, Winter 2007. pp, 24-25.

[25] Cole. Ibid, p 166.

[26] United States DoD. pp, 22-23.

[27] Kane Thomas M. Chinese Grand Strategy and Maritime Power, Frank Cass Publishers, Portland, 2002. p, 48.

[28] Cole. op cit.

[29] Cole. Ibid. United States DoD. op cit.

[30] Cole. Ibid. p, 167.

[31] The PLA Navy: A Modern Navy with Chinese Characteristics, Office of Naval Intelligence Publication, Aug 2009, p. 26.

[32] Huang Alexander Chieh-cheng, The Chinese Navy's Offshore Active Defense Strategy: Conceptualisation and Implications, Naval War College Review 47, No 3, Summer 1994. p, 13.

[33] Pehrson Christopher J, String of Pearls: Meeting the Challenge of China's Rising Power Across the Asian Littoral, US Army War College, Strategic Studies Institute, 2006. p, 3.

[34] United States DoD. Annual Report to Congress, "Military Power of the People's Republic of China 2007", p, 16.

[35] Lampton David M. The Faces of Chinese Power, Foreign Affairs 86, No 1, Jan/Feb 2007. p, 117.

[36] Pehrson. Ibid, p, 6.

[37] Lexiong Ni. Sea Power and China's Development, People's Liberation Daily available at http://www.uscc.gov/researchpapers/translated_articles/2005/05_07_18_Sea_Power_and_Chinas_Development.htm. Accessed on 08 Nov 2011.

[38] China's Navy 2007, Office of Naval Intelligence Publication, Aug 2007, p. 58.

[39] White Paper on China's National Defence in 2006 available at http://english.gov.cn/official/ 2009 01/ 20/content_1210227.htm, pp.47,23-24, accessed on 16 Sep 2011.

[40] Ibid.

[41] Shambaugh David. Modernizing China's Military, University of California Press, 2002, p 165.

[42] Cole. op cit. p, 81.

[43] China's Navy 2007. op cit, p, 11.

[44] Ibid.

[45] United States DoD. Annual Report to Congress, "Military and Security Developments Involving the People's Republic of China 2011", p, 41.

[46] Shambaugh. op cit, p, 192.

[47] Howarth Peter, China's Rising Sea Power: The PLA Navy's Submarine Challenge, Routledge Press New York, 2006. p, 69.

[48] Huang. op cit , p, 9.

[49] Shambaugh. op cit, p, 191.

[50] United States DoD. Annual Report to Congress, 2007. p. 25.

[51] Cordesman Anthony and Kleiber Martin, Chinese Military Modernization: Force Development and Strategic Capabilities, CSIS Press, Washington DC, 2007. p, 55.

[52] The PLA Navy: A Modern Navy with Chinese Characteristics. op cit, p 36.

[53] China's Navy 2007. op cit, p, 31.

[54] Cordesman and Kleiber. op cit, p 120.

[55] O'Rourke Ronald, op cit. pp, 8-9.

[56] Ibid, p, 14.

[57] Cordesman and Kleiber. op cit, p 129.

[58] Erickson Andrew S, Denmark Abraham M and Collins Gabriel. Beijing's Starter Carrier and Future Steps: Alternatives and Implications, Naval War College Review, Winter 2012, Vol 65, No 1. pp, 24-25.

[59] PLA Navy Official on Importance of Aircraft Carriers in Military Development, Zhongguo Qingnian Bao, 24 August 2007, FBIS CPP20070824710012.

[60] Erickson Andrew S, Denmark Abraham M and Collins Gabriel. op cit, p, 38.

[61] Sharma Amol, Page Jeremy, Hookway James and Pannet Rachel. Asia's New Arms Race, Wall Street Journal, Saturday Essay, 12 Feb 2011. Accessed online at http://online.wsj.com/article/ SB10001424052748704881304576094173297995198. html on 14 May 2011.

[62] Cordesman and Kleiber. op cit, p 53.

[63] Cole. op cit. p, 107.

[64] United States DoD. Annual Report to Congress, 2011. p. 30

[65] Ibid. p 28.

[66] Cole. op cit. p, 37.

[67] O'Rourke Ronald, Ibid. p, 32.

[68] Ibid, pp, 35-36.

[69] Cordesman and Kleiber. op cit, p 118.

[70] White Paper on China's National Defence in 2004 available at http:// english.gov.cn/official/ 2009 01/ 20/content_1210227.htm, pp.47,23-24, accessed on 16 Oct 2011.

[71] Corbett Julian S. Some Principles of Maritime Strategy, Dover Publications, New York, 2004. p, 56.

[72] Lexiong Ni. op cit, p, 3.

[73] Barnhart, Making it Easy for Him: The Imperial Japanese Navy and Franklin D Roosevelt to Pearl Harbour, in FDR and the US Navy, ed Marolda Edward J, St. Martin's Press, New York, 1998. pp, 36-37.

[74] Mommsen Wolfgang J. Imperial Germany 1867-1918, Arnold, London, 1995. pp, 82-83, 92-93. Berghahn VG. Germany and the Approach of War in 1914, St Martin's Press, New York, 1973. p, 32.

[75] Mommsen. Ibid. Padfield Peter. The Great Naval Race: Anglo-German Naval Rivalry 1900-1914, Birlinn Limited, Edinburgh, 1974. p, 38.

[76] Peter Lieberman. The Offense-Defense Balance, Interdependence, and War in Power and the Purse: Economic Statecraft, Interdependence and National Security, ed Jean-Marc F Blanchard, Edward D Mansfield and Norrin M Ripsman, Frank Cass Press Portland, 2000. p, 82.

[77] Barnhart. op cit 267.

[78] Gow Ian. Military Intervention in Pre-War Japanese Politics: Admiral Kato Kanji and the Washington System, Routledge, New York, 2004. pp, 138-139.

[79] Holmes James R. Mahan, a Place in the Sun and Germany's Quest for Sea Power, Comparative Strategy 23, 2004. p, 37.

[80] Shambaugh. op cit, pp, 299 and 341.

[81] Sutter Robert G. Chinese Foreign Relations: Power and Diplomacy Since the Cold War, Rowman and Littlefield, Lanham. pp, 130-131.

[82] Lexiong Ni. op cit, p, 4.

[83] Shirk Susan L. China: Fragile Superpower Oxford University Press, New York, 2007. p, 23.

[84] Ong Russell. China's Security Interests in the Post-Cold War Era, Curzon Press London, 2002. p, 182.

[85] Shirk. Ibid, p, 2.

[86] Speed Philip Andrews, Liao Xuanli and Dannreuther Roland. The Strategic Implications of China's Energy Needs, Oxford University Press, New York, 2002. p, 71.

[87] Gilpin Robert. The Political Economy of International Relations, Princeton University Press, Princeton, 1987. p, 294.

[88] Roy Denny. China's Reaction to American Predominance, Survival 45, No 3, Autumn 2003. p, 59.

[89] Sutter. op cit, p 397.

[90] Howarth. op cit, p, 173.

[91] Zweig David and Jianhai Bi. China's Global Hunt for Energy, Foreign Affairs 84, No 5, Sep/Oct 2005. p, 35.

[92] Cole Bernard D. Beijing's Strategy of Sea Denial, China Brief 6, No 23, 22 Nov 2006. p, 2.

[93] O'Rourke Ronald, China Naval Modernization: Implications for US Navy Capabilities – Background and Issues for Congress. Washington, DC: Congressional Research Service, 23 Mar 2012, pp. 3-9.

[94] Shambaugh. op cit, p, 328.

[95] Zweig and Jianhai. op cit.

[96] Hattendorf John B. What is Maritime Strategy? in Naval History and Maritime Strategy: Collected Essays, Krieger Publishing Co, Malabar, 2000. pp, 235-236.

[97] McDevitt Michael. The Strategic and Operational Context Driving PLA Navy Building, in Right Sizing the People's Liberation Army: Exploring the Contours of China's Military, Strategic Studies Institute, 2007. p, 513.

[98] Ibid.

[99] Ibid. p, 514.

[100] Ibid.

[101] Ibid.

[102] Ibid. p, 515

[103] Ibid.

[104] Ibid. p, 516.

[105] Ibid.

[106] Ibid.

Bibliography

Primary Sources

(a) Reports, Conferences and Seminars

Third Xiangshan Forum, Conducted by the China Association for Military Science, on "Evolution of International Strategic Configuration and Asia Pacific Security, Beijing, 22-24 October 2010.

The 31st United Service Institution of India National Security Seminar on "China's Quest for Global Dominance - Reality or Myth", New Delhi, 10-11 November 2010.

The 32nd United Service Institution of India National Security Seminar on "Peace and Stability in Asia Pacific Region: An Assessment of the Security Architecture", New Delhi, 17-18 November 2011.

Freedom To Use The Seas: India's Maritime Military Strategy, Integrated Headquarters of the Ministry of Defence (Navy), 2007.

Report on China's National Defence. White Paper on China's National Defence in 2004 available at http://english.gov.cn/official/ 2009 01/20/ content_1210227.htm, accessed on 16 Oct 2011.

Report on China's National Defence. White Paper on China's National Defence in 2006 available at http://www.china.org.cn/english/features/ book/194421.htm, accessed on 16 Sep 2010.

Report on China's National Defence. White Paper on China's National Defence in 2008 available at http://english.gov.cn/official/ 2009 01/ 20/ content_1210227.htm, accessed on 16 Sep 2010.

Report on China's National Defence. White Paper on China's National Defence in 2010 available at http://www.gov.cn/english/official/2005-08/17/content_24165.htm#2011, accessed on 16 Jul 2011.

Report on China's Naval Modernisation by O'Rourke Ronald, China Naval Modernization: Implications for US Navy Capabilities – Background and Issues for Congress. Washington, DC: Congressional Research Service, 12 July 2007.

Report on China's Naval Modernisation by O'Rourke Ronald, China Naval Modernization: Implications for US Navy Capabilities – Background and Issues for Congress. Washington, DC: Congressional Research Service, 26 August 2011.

Report on China's Naval Modernisation by O'Rourke Ronald, China Naval Modernization: Implications for US Navy Capabilities – Background and Issues for Congress. Washington, DC: Congressional Research Service, 29 May 2009.

Report on China's Naval Modernisation by O'Rourke Ronald, China Naval Modernization: Implications for US Navy Capabilities – Background and Issues for Congress. Washington, DC: Congressional Research Service, 23 Mar 2012.

Report on China's Security by NIDS. China Security Report, National Institute of Defence Studies, Japan, March 2011.

Report on Energy Information. US Energy Information Administration / International Energy Outlook 2010.

Report on Global Trends 2025 by National Intelligence Council. Global Trends 2025: A Transformed World, US ONI, Nov 2008.

Report on India's Annual Trade Statistics 2010 by Department of Commerce, Government of India, Export Import Data Bank available at http://commerce.nic.in/eidb/iecnt.aspIbid, accessed on 21 Jul 2011.

Report on India's Annual Trade Statistics 2010 by Government of India, Ministry of Commerce available at http://commerce.nic.in/eidb/default.asp accessed on 08 Nov 2010.

Report on PLA Navy. The PLA Navy: A Modern Navy with Chinese Characteristics, Office of Naval Intelligence Publication, Aug 2009.

Report on Statistical Abstract of Transportation and Communications of

Republic of China 2008. China. Department of Statistics.Ministry of Transportation. China: Department of Statistics, Ministry of Transportation, 2009.

Report on Water Security of India by IDSA Task Force. Water Security for India: The External Dynamics, IDSA, 2010.

Report on World Population 2300. United Nations.World Population to 2300.Department of Economic and Social Affairs, Population Division.

Report to US Congress. United States DoD. Annual Report to Congress, "Military and Security Developments Involving the People's Republic of China 2011".

Report to US Congress. United States DoD. Annual Report to Congress, "Military Power of the People's Republic of China 2009".

Report to US Congress. United States DoD. Annual Report to Congress, Military Power of the People's Republic of China 2007.

Report on KailashMansarovarYatra by Ministry of External Affairs, Government of India available at http://www.mea.gov.in/ mystart.php?id=8900, accessed on 21 Jul 2011.

(b) Newspapers, Magazines, Periodicals and Year Books

Armed Forces Year Book, New Delhi.

Brahmand Year Book, New Delhi.

Janes Fighting Ships, London

SIPRI Year Book, Stockholm.

SPs Military Year Book, New Delhi.

Strategic Analysis, New Delhi.

Strategic Digest, New Delhi.

The 2010 Legatum Prosperity Index Brochure. Legatum Institute.

The 2010 Legatum Prosperity Index Full Report. Legatum Institute.

The 2011 Legatum Prosperity Index Brochure. Legatum Institute.

The 2011 Legatum Prosperity Index Full Report. Legatum Institute.

The 2012 Legatum Prosperity Index Brochure. Legatum Institute.

The 2012 Legatum Prosperity Index Full Report. Legatum Institute.

The Military Balance 2010.The International Institute for Strategic Studies, London.

The Military Balance 2011.The International Institute for Strategic Studies, London.

The Military Balance 2019.The International Institute for Strategic Studies, London.

(c) Websites

http://china-pla.blogspot.com.

http://commerce.nic.in.

http://en.wikipedia.org/wiki/China.

http://english.cri.cn

http://indiabudget.nic.in.

http://meaindia.nic.in.

http://mod.nic.in.

http://online.wsj.com

http://petroleum.nic.in.

http://shipping.nic.in.

http://the-diplomat.com

http://www.business-standard.com

http://www.businessweek.com

http://www.cceec.com.cn/English

http://www.defence.org.cn.

http://www.eai.doe.gov.

http://www.fas.org.

http://www.foreignpolicy.com

http://www.globalsecurity.org.

http://www.globaltimes.com.

http://www.idoer.org.

http://www.nti.org.

http://www.rand.org/pubs/testimonies

http://www.sinodefence.com.

http://www.telegraph.co.uk/news/worldnews/asia/china.html

http://www.top81.cn.

http://www.un.org.

http://www.uscc.gov/researchpapers/translated

Secondary Sources

(a) Articles

Agnihotri Kamlesh Kumar, Strategic Direction of the PLA Navy: Capability and Intent Assessment, Maritime Affairs Vol 6 No 1, Summer 2010.

Ahmed Ali, A Consideration of Sino-Indian Conflict, IDSA Issue Brief, 24 October 2011.

Aiyengar SRR Lt Gen (Retd), A Perspective on India-China Relations, CLAWS Journal, Summer 2010.

Singh Amit. South China Sea Dispute: A New Area of Global Tension. NMF Commentary. 2011

Angang Hu and Honghua Men, The Rising of Modern China: Comprehensive National Power and Grand Strategy, Strategy and Management No 3, 2002.

ASEAN and the Indian Ocean, Bateman Sam, Chan Jane and Graham Euan (ed), RSIS Policy Paper, 2011.

Asia's Balance of Power: China's Military Rise; There Are Ways to Reduce the Threat to Stability That an Emerging Superpower Poses, available at http://www.economist.com/node/21552193 accessed on 08 April 2012.

Bakshi GDMaj Gen (Retd). The Chinese Threat in Perspective, CLAWS Journal, Summer 2010.

Barnett Roger W, Strategic Culture and it Relationship to Naval Strategy, Naval War College Review 60, No 1, Winter 2007.

Bickford Thomas J, Holz Heidi A and Vellucci Frederic Jr, Uncertain Waters: Thinking About China's Emergence as a Maritime Power, CNA China Studies, September 2011.

Bijian Zheng, "A New Path for China's Peaceful Rise and the Future of Asia," speech to the Bo'ao forum for Asia, April 2003, reproduced in China's Peaceful Rise: Speeches of Zheng Bijian 1997-2005. Brookings Institution Press. Washington DC. 2005.

Bijian Zheng. "China's Peaceful Rise to Great-Power Status." Foreign Affairs 84, September/October 2005

Bitzinger Richard A, The China Syndrome: Chinese Military Modernisation and the Rearming of Southeast Asia, RSIS Working Paper No 126, 02 May 2007.

Chandrashekar S, et al. China's Anti-ship Ballistic Missile Game Changer in the Pacific Ocean. International Strategic and Security Studies Programme, NIAS, Bangalore, November 2011.

Chang Amy and Doston John. Indigenous Weapons Development in China's Military Modernisation, US China Economic and Security Review Commission Staff Research Report, 05 April 2012.

Chang Felix K, China's Naval Rise and the South China Sea: An Operational Assessment, Foreign Policy Research Institute, Orbis, Winter 2012.

Chang Felix K. China's Naval Rise and the South China Sea: An Operational Assessment, Foreign Policy Research Institute Journal, Winter 2012.

Chase Micheal S and Erickson Andrew S.The Jamestown Foundation. China Brief Volume: 9 Issue 19. 24 Sept 2009.

Chen YanMaj Gen. Commissar of the 5th Naval Escort Fleet Shares Stories at CRI, available at http://english.cri.cn/6909/2010/12/23/1361s611657.htm, accessed on 24 Dec 2010.

Cheng Dean, China's View of South Asia and the Indian Ocean, Heritage Lectures No 1163, 18 March 2010.

Cheng Dean, Sea Power and the Chinese State: China's Maritime Ambitions, Heritage Backgrounder No 2576, 11 July 2011.

China Analysis Brief.Available at http://www.eia.gov/EMEU/cabs/China/pdf.pdf.Accessed on 27 August 2011.

China Brief, Vol X Issue 12, The Jamestown Foundation, 11 June 2010.

China Brief, Vol X Issue 15, The Jamestown Foundation, 22 July 2010.

China Brief, Vol X Issue 18, The Jamestown Foundation, 10 September 2010.

China Brief, Vol X Issue 19, The Jamestown Foundation, 24 September 2010.

China Brief, Vol XI Issue 2, The Jamestown Foundation, 28 January 2011.

China Brief, Vol XI Issue 20, The Jamestown Foundation, 28 October 2011.

China Brief, Vol XI Issue 23, The Jamestown Foundation, 21 December 2011.

China Brief, Vol XI Issue 6, The Jamestown Foundation, 08 April 2011.

China Brief, Vol XII Issue 1, The Jamestown Foundation, 06 January 2012.

China Brief, Vol XII Issue 2, The Jamestown Foundation, 20 January 2012.

China Brief, Vol XII Issue 3, The Jamestown Foundation, 03 February 2012.

China Brief, Vol XII Issue 4, The Jamestown Foundation, 21 February 2012.

China Brief, Vol XII Issue 5, The Jamestown Foundation, 02 March 2012.

China Brief, Vol XII Issue 6, The Jamestown Foundation, 15 March 2012.

China Brief, Vol XII Issue 7, The Jamestown Foundation, 30 March 2012.

China Brief, Vol XII Issue 8, The Jamestown Foundation, 12 April 2012.

ChinaCambodia, and the Five Principles of Peaceful Coexistence. Richardson Sophie. New York: Columbia University Press, 2010.

China Economic Forecast to 2040 and Defence Budgets available at http://www.globalsecurity.com/2010/03/china-economic-forecast-to-2040-and.html accessed on 08 Nov 2010.

China News Digest, Institute for Defence Studies and Analyses, No 3, June 2011.

China News Digest, Institute for Defence Studies and Analyses, No 2, May 2011.

China News Digest, Institute for Defence Studies and Analyses, No 1, March 2011.

China News Digest, Institute for Defence Studies and Analyses, No 4, July 2011.

China News Digest, Institute for Defence Studies and Analyses, No 6/7, September/October 2011.

China-CNPC, China-Myanmar Oil and Gas Pipeline. Project report available at http://www.cceec.com.cn/English/Project/China/2010/0914/8530.html, accessed on 12 Aug 2011.HerbergMikkal E. Pipeline Politics in Asia. NBR Special Report 23, Sept 2010.

Cole Bernard D. Beijing's Strategy of Sea Denial, China Brief 6, No 23, 22 Nov 2006.

Cole Bernard. China's Naval Modernisation: Cause for Storm Warnings. NDU Symposia 2010.

Cooper Cortez A. The PLA Navy's New Historic Missions. RAND Testimony CT 332, Jun 2009. available at http://www.rand.org/pubs/testimonies/CT332/. Accessed on 09 Sep 2010.

Cordner Lee, Progressing Maritime Security Cooperation in the Indian Ocean, Naval War College Review Vol 64 No 4, Autumn 2011.

Dali Yang and Hong Zhao. The Rise of India: China's Perspectives and

Responses, available at http://www.daliyang.com/files/ Yang_and_Zhao_The_Rise_of_India- China_ s_perspectives_and _reponse. pdf accessed on 09 Dec 2010.

Dannreuther Ronald, China and Global Oil: Vulnerability and Opportunity, International Affairs, 2011.

David C Evans and Mark R. Peattie, Kaigun: Strategy, Tactics, and Technology in the Imperial Japanese Navy, 1887-1941, Naval Institute Press, Annapolis, 1997. .

Dragonette Charles N. The Dragon At Sea-China's Maritime Enterprise, US Naval Institute Proceedings, 107, 05May 1981.

DuttaSujit, Managing and Engaging Rising China: India's Evolving Posture, CSIS, The Washington Quarterly, Spring 2011.

Dutton Peter, Three Disputes and Three Objectives: China and the South China Sea, Naval War College Review Vol 64 No 4, Autumn 2011.

Economy of the People's Republic of China. Available at http:// en.wikipedia.org/wiki/Economy_ of_the_ People's_Republic_of_China. Accessed on 20 August 2011.

Erickson Andrew S and Collins Gabriel, China's Maritime Evolution: Military and Commercial Factors, Pacific Focus, Vol XXII No 2, Fall 2007.

Erickson Andrew S and Collins Gabriel. China's Maritime Evolution: Military and Commercial factors. Pacific Focus, Vol XXII, No 2, Fall 2007.

Erickson Andrew S and Yang David, Using the Land to Control the Sea, Naval War College Review, Vol 62 No 4, Autumn 2009.

Erickson Andrew S, Denmark Abraham M and Collins Gabriel. Beijing's Starter Carrier and Future Steps: Alternatives and Implications, Naval War College Review, Winter 2012, Vol 65, No 1.

Fernando Sithara Dr YJ, China's Maritime Relations With South Asia: From Confrontation to Cooperation Part 1, Future Directions International, Strategic Analysis Paper, 24 November 2010.

Fernando Sithara Dr YJ, China's Maritime Relations With South Asia: From

Confrontation to Cooperation Part 2, Future Directions International, Strategic Analysis Paper, 26 November 2010.

Godwin Paul HB, China's Defence Modernisation: Aspirations and Capabilities, Asian Perspectives on the Challenges of China.Paper presented at the Institute for National Strategic Studies' (INSS) Annual Asia-Pacific Symposium, 07-08 March 2000.

Goh Evelyn, Rising Power...To Do What? Evaluating China's Power in Southeast Asia, RSIS Working Paper No 226, 30 March 2011.

Goldstein Avery, The Diplomatic Face of China's Grand Strategy: A Rising Power's Emerging Choice, The China Quarterly, 2001.

Grant Charles. India's Response to China's Rise. Centre for European Reform, Issue Brief, 2010.

Guanglie Liang, Chinese Defence Minister. China Preparing for Conflict in Every Direction, as quoted in Beijing News Net, available at http:// www.telegraph.co.uk/news/worldnews/asia/china.html accessed on 29 Dec 2010.

HaiderZiad, "Baluchis, Beijing, and Pakistan's Gwadar Port," Georgetown Journal of International Affairs 6, Winter/Spring 2005.

Hayoun Jessie Ryou, "The Meaning of China's 'Peaceful Development' Concept, ORF Occasional Paper 12, Nov 2009.

Holmes James R, Soft Power at Sea: Zheng He and Chinese Maritime Diplomacy, High Beam Research Article, 01 January 2006.

Holmes James R. India Looking East.The Diplomat, Flash Points, 20 Sep 2011, available at http://the-diplomat.com/flashpoints-blog/2011/09/20/ india-looking-east/ accessed on 20 Sep 2011.

Holmes James R. Mahan, a Place in the Sun and Germany's Quest for Sea Power.Comparative Strategy, 2004.

Holmes James. China's Maritime Strategy is More Than Naval Strategy. The Jamestown Foundation. China Brief Volume: 11 Issue 6. 08 April 2011.

Holslag Jonathan, Embracing Chinese Global Security Ambitions, CSIS, The Washington Quarterly, July 2009.

Huang Alexander Chieh-cheng, The Chinese Navy's Offshore Active Defense Strategy: Conceptualisation and Implications, Naval War College Review 47, No 3, Summer 1994.

Huang Yukon, Reinterpreting China's Success Through the New Economic Geography, Carnegie Papers, Asia Programme No 15, November 2010.

Ji You and Kia Chee, China's Naval Deployment to Somalia and its Implications, EAI Background Brief No 454, 29 May 2009.

Jiabao Wen, "Turning Your Eyes to China," speech on 10 December 2003, transcript available in the Harvard Gazette Archives.available at http://www.hno.harvard.edu/gazette/2003/12.11/10-wenspeech. Html. Accessed on 05 March 2011.

Joseph TD GpCapt, Military Modernisation in China: Some Implications for India, Air Power Journal Vol 3 No 1 Spring 2006 (January-March).

KanwalGurmeet Brig (Retd), India-China Strategic Relations Further Improvement is Contigent on Resolution of the Territorial Dispute, CLAWS Journal, Summer 2010.

KapilaSubhash Dr, China's Defence Budget 2012: Implications for India's Security Analysed, Paper No 4964, 15 March 2012.

KapilaSubhash Dr. Asian Security Environment and Choices for India, Synergy, CENJOWS, January 2010.

Kaplan Robert D, The Geography of Chinese Power: How Far Can Beijing Reach on Land and at Sea? Foreign Affairs, May/June 2010.

KatakeyRakteem and Duce John. India Loses to China in Global Race to Secure Energy Assets, available at http://oilandglory.foreignpolicy.com/category/region/ south_asia accessed on 07 Sep 2010.

Katoch PC Lt Gen (Retd). China:A Threat or Challenge, CLAWS Journal, Summer 2010.

Lampton David M. The Faces of Chinese Power, Foreign Affairs 86, No 1,

Jan/Feb 2007.

Lexiong Ni. Sea Power and China's Development, People's Liberation Daily available at http://www.uscc.gov/researchpapers/translated_articles/ 2005/05_07_18_Sea_Power_and_Chinas_Development.htm.Accessed on 08 Nov 2011.

Li Cheng, The Battle for China's Top Nine Leadership Posts, CSIS, The Washington Quarterly, Winter 2012.

Li Zhang. China-India Relations: Strategic Engagement and Challenges, Centre for Asian Studies, IFRI, Sep 2010.

Linn Jenny, China's Energy Security Dilemma, Project 2049 Institute, Futuregram 12-001.

Mackenzie Peter W, Red Crosses Blue Water, Hospital Ships and China's Expanding Naval Presence, CNA China Studies, September 2011.

McDevitt Michael, China's Naval Modernisation: Cause for Storm Warnings, 2010 Pacific Symposium, INSS, NDU, 16 June 2010.

Mearsheimer John. The Gathering Storm: China's Challenge to U.S. Power in Asia Fourth Annual Michael Hintze Lecture in International Security, 04 August 2010.

Mehta Sureesh Admiral, Changing Roles of Navies in the Contemporary World Order with Specific Reference to the Indian Navy, Journal of Defence Studies Vol 3 No 2, April 2009.

Mehta Sureesh Admiral, Chief of the Naval Staff. In an address to the Defence Services Staff College, Wellington on 04 April 2008.

Michael Mazza. Chess on the High Seas: Dangerous Times for US China Relations, AEI Newsletter No 3, Aug 2010.

Mike MullenAdmiral, Chairman of the Joint Chiefs of Staff. Address to the Asia Society in Washington on 10 June 2010, available at http:// www.businessweek.com/news/2010-06-10/u-s-concern-over-china-military-growing-mullen-says-update1-.html accessed on 11 Jun 2010.

Mingjiang Li, China's Rising Maritime Aspirations: Impact on Good Neighbour

Policy, RSIS Commentaries No 053/2012 dated 28 March 2012.

Mingjiang Li, Rising From Within: China's Search for a Multilateral World and its Implications for Sino-US Relations, RSIS Working Paper No 225, 25 March 2011.

Mohan Raja C, India and the Changing Geopolitics of the Indian Ocean, NMF Eminent Persons Lecture Series, 19 July 2010.

Mohan Raja C, Maritime Power: India and China Turn to Mahan, ISAS Working Paper No 71, 07 July 2009.

Mohan Raja C. Power and Paradox: The Future of Sino-Indian Relations, Think India Quarterly, Vol13, No 2, Apr-Jun 2010.

Nakai Aki, China's Naval Modernisation: Reflections on a Symposium, Boston University Occasional Papers on Asia, 01 February 2011.

PalitParamaSinha. China's Soft Power in Asia, RSIS Working Paper No 200, 08 Jun 2010,

Pandey Dr. SheoNandan. Coping with the Rise of China: Imperatives for South Asia, ISPSW Journal, Jan 2011, p. 6, available at http://www.isn.ethz.ch/isn/Digital-Library/Publications/Detail /?id =125885, accessed on 05 Jan 2011.

People's Liberation Army Navy–History, available at http://www.globalsecurity.org/ military/world/ china/plan-history.htm, accessed on 09 Dec 2010.

PLA Navy Official on Importance of Aircraft Carriers in Military Development, ZhongguoQingnianBao, 24 August 2007, FBIS CPP20070824710012.

Premvir Das Vice Admiral (Retd). The Great Chinese Quest, available at http://www.business-standard.com /india/news/premvir-dasgreat-chinese-quest/399408/ accessed on 28 Jun 2010.

Qi Xu, Maritime Geostrategy and the Development of the Chinese Navy in the Early Twenty-First Century, Naval War College Review 59, Autumn 2006.

RajagopalanRajeshwariPillai and Prasad Kailash, Sino-Indian Border Infrastucture: Issues and Challenges, ORF Issue Brief No 23, August 2010.

Rajan DS, China: The Unfolding Asia-Pacific Strategy, Chennai Centre for China Studies, Paper No 873, 04 October 2011.

Raman B, Chinese Navy's Power Projection, South Asia Analysis Group, Paper No 3780, 27 April 2010.

RanadeJayadeva. China's Recent Policy of Assertiveness, Centre for air Power Studies Issue Brief 34/10, 12 Nov 2010.

Ross Robert S. The Rise of Chinese Power and Implications for Regional Security Order, Orbis, Foreign Policy Research Institute, Fall 2010.

Roy Bhaskar, An India China Military Conflict Part 1, South Asia Analysis Group, Paper No 4903, 09 February 2012.

Roy Bhaskar, An India China Military Conflict Part 2, South Asia Analysis Group, Paper No 4904, 09 February 2012.

Roy Bhaskar, China: PLA's Great Grab, South Asia Analysis Group, Paper No 4806, 07 December 2011.

Roy Bhaskar, China: Stretching To the Indian Ocean, South Asia Analysis Group, Paper No 4814, 13 December 2011.

Roy Denny. China's Reaction to American Predominance, Survival 45, No 3, Autumn 2003.

RyouHayoun Jessie, the Meaning of China's Peaceful Development Concept, ORF Occasional Paper No 12, November 2009.

Shambaugh David, Coping With a Conflicted China, CSIS, The Washington Quarterly, Winter 2011.

SharanVivan and Thiller Nicole, Oil Supply routes in the Asia Pacific: China's Strategic Calculations, ORF Occasional Paper No 24, September 2011.

Sharma Amol, Page Jeremy, Hookway James and Pannet Rachel.Asia's New Arms Race, Wall Street Journal, Saturday Essay, 12 Feb 2011.Accessed online at http://online.wsj.com/article/

SB10001424052748704881304576094173297995198.html on 14 May 2011.

SiddiquiHuma. The Financial Express: Krishna to take up Growing Trade Defeciet with China, available at http://www.financialexpress.com/news/ krishna-to-take-up-growing-trade-deficit-with-china/599870/ accessed on 06 Sep 2010.

Singh Mandip and Kumar Lalit, China's Defence Budget 2012: An Analysis, IDSA Issue Brief, 28 March 2012.

Stevens Paul. Oil and Gas Pipelines: Prospects and Problems. NBR Special Report 23, Sept 2010.

Subrahmanyam K. Countering China's New Assertiveness available at http:/ /business-standard.com/ india/storypage.php?autono=406992 accessed on 07 Sep 2010.

Swaine Michael D and Tellis Ashley J. Interpreting China's Grand Strategy: Past, Present and Future. RAND Research Brief. MR-1121-AF, 2000.

Swaine Michael D. China's Assertive Behaviour, China Leadership Monitor, No 34, Fall 2010.

Tellis Ashley J, Dr. China's Grand Strategy, CLAWS Journal, Summer 2010.

ThapliyalSheruMaj Gen.PLA's New Mantra- Building Capabilities, AGNI Vol. XII. No III, 2011.

The Dragon's New Teeth: A Rare Look Inside the World's Biggest Military Expansion, available at http://www.economist.com/node/ 21552193accessed on 08 April 2012.

Valencia Mark J, Foreign Military Activities in Asian EEZs: Conflict Ahead, NBR Special Report No 27, May 2011.

Vasan RS Cmde (Retd), China's Force Multipliers, South Asia Analysis Group, Paper No 4960, 13 March 2012.

Vasan RS Cmde (Retd), China's Maritime Ambitions: Implications for Regional Security, South Asia Analysis Group, Paper No 4281, 17 January 2011.

Walker Philip, Beijing's Blue Water Navy – Is China Building an Empire on the Sea, Foreign Policy, 03 June 2011.

WeijieGao, "Development Strategy of Chinese Shipping Company under the Multilateral Framework of WTO" speech to the International Maritime Forum 2003, Available at http://www.cosco.com.cn/ en/pic/ forum/654923323232.pdf. accessed on 20 August 2011.

Yinchu Tang, An Exploration of China's Nucleus National Interests, International Strategic Studies, 3rd Issue, 2010.

Yoshihara Toshi and Holmes James R, Can China Defend a Core Interest in the South China Sea, CSIS, The Washington Quarterly, Spring 2011.

Yu Huming, Marine Fishery Management in China, Marine Policy, 15, 01Jan 1991.

Yung Christopher D, Rustici Ross, Kardon Isaac and Wiseman Joshua, China's Out of Area Naval Operations: Case Studies Trajectories Obstacles and Potential Solutions, INSS Chian Strategic Perspectives No 3, December 2010.

Wikipedia.China and the United Nations, available at http://en.wikipedia.org/ wiki/China_and_the_ United_Nations, accessed on 07 Sep 2010.

Zweig David and Jianhai Bi. China's Global Hunt for Energy, Foreign Affairs 84, No 5, Sep/Oct 2005.

(b)   Books

Bicknell Jane, Dodman David and Satterthwaite David (ed), Adapting Cities to Climate Change: Understanding and Addressing the Development Challenges, Earthscan,London, 2009.

BardhanPranab,Awakening Giants Feet of Clay: Assessing the Economic Rise of China and India, Oxford University Press, New Delhi, 2010.

Barnhart, Making it Easy for Him: The Imperial Japanese Navy and Franklin D Roosevelt to Pearl Harbour, in FDR and the US Navy, edMarolda Edward J, St. Martin's Press, New York, 1998.

Halper Stefan,Beijing Consensus: How China's Authoritarian Model Will

Dominate the Twenty-first Century,Basic Books, New York, 2010.

Bergamini David. Japan's Imperial Conspiracy, Heinemann, London, 1971.

Asad-UlIqbalLatif, Between Rising Powers: China Singapore and India. ISEASPublishing, Singapore, 2007.

ModiRenu (ed), Beyond Relocation: the Imperative of Sustainable Resettlement, Sage Publications,New Delhi, 2009.

Bisley Nick. Building Asia's Security.International Institute for Strategic Studies, Routledge, 2009.

Claude Arpi, Born In Sin - The Panchsheel Agreement, Mittal Publications, New Delhi, 2004.

Li Lanqing,Breaking Through: the Birth of China's Opening UpPolicy, Oxford University Press, Oxford, 2009.

BisleyNick,Building Asia's Security, Routeledge, 2009.

Balme Stephanie and Dowdle Michael W (ed),Building Constitutionalism in China, Palgrave Macmillan,New York, 2009.

Mohan Malik, China and India - Great Power Rivals, First Forum Press, London, 2011.

Marlene Laruelle and BayramBalcied, China and India in Central Asia, Palgrave MacMillan, 2010.

Sharma Shalendra D, China and India in the Age of Globalisation.Cambridge University Press, New Delhi, 2009.

Jonathan Holslag,China and India-Prospects for Peace, Columbia University Press, 2010.

KondapalliSrikanth and Emi MifuneChina and Its Neighbours, Pentagon Press, 2010.

Garrison Jean A,China and the Energy Equation in Asia: the Determinants of Policy Choice: FirstForumPress,Colorado,2009.

Keith Ronald C,China From the Inside Out: Fitting the People's Republic into the World, Pluto PressLondon, 2009.

Ellis R Evan,China in Latin America: the What and WhereFores, Lynne Rienner Publishers, Boulder,2009.

Pablos Patricia Ordonez de and LytrasMiltiadis D (ed).,China Information Technology Handbook, Springer, New York 2009.

Blankert Jan Willem,China Rising: Will the West be Able to Cope, World Scientific Publishing, Singapore,2009.

Dittmer Lowell and George T Yu (ed). , Chinathe Developing World and the New Global Dynamic, Lynne Rienner Publishers, London,2010.

Rosemary Foot and Andrew Walter,China The United States And Global Order, Cambridge University Press, 2011.

AdhikariPushpaDr,China Threat in South Asia, Lancer, Delhi, 2012.

Mackerras Colin and Clarke Michael (ed),China Xinjiang and Central Asia: History Transition and Cross Border Interaction Into the 21st Century.Routledge, London,2009.

TripathiDr NK,China's Asia Pacific Strategy and India, Vij Books, 2010.

Richard D Fisher Jr,China's Military Modernization, Praeger Security International, 2008.

China's Military Power, US DOD, Manas Publications, 2010.

China's Navy 2007, Office of Naval Intelligence Publication, Aug 2007.

Jagannath P Panda,China's Path to Power, Pentagon Security International, 2010.

Phadke Ramesh Air Cmde, China's Power Projection, Manas Publications, 2005.

Singh BKP,China's Tibet Policy, Sumit Enterprises, 2009.

ChansoriaMonika, China-Military Modernisation and Security, Knowledge World Publishers, New Delhi, 2011.

Clegg Jenny,China's Global Strategy: Towards a Multipolar World. Pluto Press, London,2009.

Jeffreys Elaine (ed).,China's Governmentalities: Governing Change Changing Government.Routledge, London,2009.

Mingjiang Li (ed).,China's International Relations in Asia: Critical Issues in Modern Politics.Routledge, London,2009.

Fisher Richard D. Westport,China's Military Modernisation: Building for Regional and Global Reach, Pentagon Press, 2009.

USDepartment of Defence,China's Military Power,Manas Publications, New Delhi,2010.

ZhuZhiqun,China's New Diplomacy: Rationale Strategic and Significance,Ashgate, Surrey,2010.

PandaJagannath P,China's Path to Power: Party Military and the Politics of State Transition, Pentagon Security International, New Delhi, 2010.

IidaMasafumi (ed).,China's Shift: Global Strategy of the Rising Power. NIDS, Toyko, 2009.

Das Gautam,China-Tibet-India : the 1962 War and the Strategic Military Future,Haranand Publishers, New Delhi 2009.

Blasko Dennis J,Chinese Army Today: Tradition and Transformation for the 21st Century,Routledge, London,2010.

Lanteigne Marc,Chinese Foreign Policy: an Introduction,Routledge, New York,2009.

Anthony H Cordesman and Martin Kleiber,Chinese Military Modernisation - Force Development and Strategic Capabilities, The CSIS Press, 2010.

Chen YaTien,Chinese Military Theory - Ancient and Modern, Mosaic Press, 1992.

Gries Peter Hays and Rosen Stanley (ed).,Chinese Politics: State Society and the Market,Routledge, London,2010.

Gries Peter Hays, Rosen, Stanley (ed).,Chinese Politics: Staten Society and the Market,Routledge , London 2010.

Ross Robert S,Chinese Security Policy: Structure Power and

Politics,Routledge, London,2009.

Chansoria Monika,Chinese WMD Proliferation in Asia: US Response, KW Publishers, New Delhi2009.

Christopher Pehrson J, String of Pearls: Meeting the Challenge of China's Rising Power Across the Asian Littoral, US Army War College, Strategic Studies Institute, 2006.

Cole Bernard D. The Great Wall at Sea: China's Navy Enters the Twenty-first Century, Annapolis: Naval Institute Press, 2001.

Barry Sautman and June TeufelDreyers,Contemporary Tibet - Politics, Development and Society In A Disputed Region, Pentagon Press, 2008.

Corbett Julian S, Some Principles of Maritime Strategy, Naval Institute Press, Annapolis, 1988.

Corbett Julian S. Some Principles of Maritime Strategy, Dover Publications, New York, 2004.

Cordesman Anthony and Kleiber Martin, Chinese Military Modernization: Force Development and Strategic Capabilities, CSIS Press, Washington DC, 2007.

JhaPrem Shankar, Crouching Dragon Hidden Tiger: Can China and India Dominate the West, Soft Skull Press, New York 2010.

Lai Hongyi,Domestic Source of China's Foreign Policy: Regimes Leadership Prioritiesand Process,Routledge,London2010.

Mathew John,Dragon Unraveled, Pentagon Press, Delhi 2011.

DuttaSujit, Pollock Jonathan D and Yang Micheal L (ed), China's Emerging Power and Military Role: Implications for South Asia, In China's Shadow: Regional Perspectives on Chinese Foreign Policy and Military Development, RAND, 2002.

Reddy B Sudhakara (ed), Economic Reforms in India and China: Emerging Issues and Challenges, Sage Publication, New Delhi,2009.

Bruce Swanson, Eighth Voyage of the Dragon - A History of China's Quest for Sea Power, Naval Institute Press, Annapolis 1982.

Ed Mohan Guruswamy,Emerging Trends In Indo-China Relations, Hope India Publications, 2006.

SugandhaEvolution Of Maritime Strategy And National Security Of India, Decent Books, New Delhi, 2008.

Fairbank John King and Goldman Merle, China: A New History, Cambridge, MA, Harvard University Press, 1996.

Fisher Jr Richard D. China's Military Modernization, Praeger Security International, 2008.

Friedberg Aaron L,Hegemony withChinese Characteristicsin a Contest forSupremacy: China, America and the Struggle for Mastery in Asia, WW Norton and Company, August 2011.

Gilpin Robert. The Political Economy of International Relations, Princeton University Press, Princeton, 1987.

Gilpin Robert. War and Change in World Politics, Cambridge University Press, New York, 1981.

Paus Eva, Prime Penelope B and WesternJon (ed).,Global Giant: Is China Changing the Rules of the Game, Palgrave Macmillan, New York 2009.

Kanbur Ravi and ZhangXiaobo (ed).,Governing Rapid Growth in China: Equity and Institutions,Routledge, London 2009.

Gow Ian, Military Intervention in Pre-War Japanese Politics: Admiral Kato Kanji and the Washington System, Routledge, New York, 2004.

Gray Colin S, The Leverage of Sea Power, The Free Press, New York, 1992.

Jean C Oi, Rozelle Scott and Zhou Xueguang (ed), Growing Pains: Tensions and Opportunity in China's Transformation, Walter H Shorenstein Asia-Pacific Research Centre, Stanford,2010.

GuoSujian. "Challenges and Opportunities for China's 'Peaceful Rise'," in China's Peaceful Rise in the 21st Century: Domestic and International Conditions, ed. SujianGuo. Ashgate, Aldershot, 2006.

Hattendorf John B. What is Maritime Strategy? in Naval History and Maritime Strategy: Collected Essays, Krieger Publishing Co, Malabar, 2000.

Hobson Rolf, Imperialism at Sea: Naval Strategic Thought, the Ideology of Sea Power and the Tirpitz Plan, 1875-1914, Brill Academic Publishers, Boston, 2002.

Howarth Peter, China's Rising Sea Power: The PLA Navy's Submarine Challenge, Routledge Press New York, 2006.

Hsu Immanuel CY,The Rise of Modern China, Oxford University Press, 2000.

Huntington Samuel P, The Clash of Civilizations and the Remaking of World Order, Touchstone, New York,1996.

Imperial Germany 1867-1918, Politics Culture and Society in an Authoritarian State, Wolfgang J Mommsen, Arnold, London, 1995.

Ed Gurudas Das, C Joshua Thomas,India - China: Trade And Strategy For Frontier Development, Bookwell, New Delhi, 2011.

Prem Shankar Jha, India and China - The Battle Between Hard and Soft Power, Penguin, 2010.

SikdarBimal Kumar and Sikdar Amitabh,India and China: Strategic Energy Management and Security,Manas Publications, New Delhi,2009.

JhaPrem Shankar,India and China: The Battle BetweenSoft and Hard Power, Penguin Books, New Delhi,2010.

Ed Ira Pande,India China Neighbours Strangers, , Harper Collins Publishers, India, 2010.

Guruswamy Mohan and ZorawarDauletSingh,India China Relations: the Border Issue and Beyond, Viva Books, New Delhi,2009.

Indian Naval Strategy In The Twenty First Century, James R Holmes, Andrew C Winner, Toshi Yoshihara, Routledge, 2009.

Ed DS Rajan,Indian Perspectives on China, TR Publications, 2010.

Integrated Headquarters of Ministry of Defence (Navy), Freedom to Use the Seas: India's Maritime Military Strategy, 2007.

Culas Christian and Robinne Francois (ed).,Inter-ethnic Dynamics in Asia: Considering the Other Through Ethnonyms Territories and Rituals,Routledge , Oxon 2010.

David Bergamini,Japan's Imperial Conspiracy, Heinemann, London, 1971.

Peerenboom Randall (ed).,Judicial Independence in China: Lessons for Global Rule of Law Promotion,Cambridge University Press, Cambridge, 2010.

Kane Thomas M, Chinese Grand Strategy and Maritime Power, Frank Cass Publishers, Portland, 2002.

Kaplan Robert D, China's arrival: China's Two-Ocean Strategy, Centre for a New American Security (CNAS), Washington, 2009.

Kaplan Robert D, South Asia's Geography of Conflict, Centre for a New American Security (CNAS), Washington, August 2010.

Lai David. US-China Relations: A New Start, in The People's Liberation Army and China in Transition, ed Flanagan Stephen J and Marti Michael E, NDU Press, Washington DC, 2003.

Lee John. Will China Fail, Federation Press, 2007.

Liu Xuecheng. China's Strategic Culture and its Political Dynamics. The Rise of China, Pentagon Press, 2008.

Luttwak Edward. The Political Uses of Sea Power. Johns Hopkins University Press, Baltimore, 1974.

Jonathan Clements,Makers of The Modern World, Haus Publishing Ltd, 2008.

JhaPremShankar,Managed Chaos: the Fragility of the Chinese Miracle, Sage Publications, New Delhi2009.

Massie Robert K, Dreadnought: Britain, Germany and the Coming of the Great War, Ballantine Books, New York, 1991.

Levathes Louise. When China Ruled the Seas, Oxford University Press, 1994.

Lhasa-Streets with Memories, Robert Barnett, Columbia University Press, 2006.

McDevitt Michael. The Strategic and Operational Context Driving PLA Navy Building, in Right Sizing the People's Liberation Army: Exploring the Contours of China's Military, Strategic Studies Institute, 2007.

Sujeet Samadar, Cmde (Retd), USI,Minerals, Markets and Maritime Strategy, Vij Books, 2011.

Ed SandhuMaj Gen PJS,Mishra Brajesh- Keynote Address, China's Quest for Global Dominance: Reality or Myth,Vij Books, New Delhi. 2011.

GrassoJune,CorrinJay and Kort Michael,Modernisation and Revolution in China: from the Opium Wars to the Olympics, 4th ed., ME Sharpe, New York 2009.

David Shambaugh, Modernizing China's Military, University of California Press, 2002.

Mommsen Wolfgang J, Imperial Germany 1867-1918, Arnold, London, 1995. pp, 82-83, 92-93. Berghahn VG. Germany and the Approach of War in 1914, St Martin's Press, New York, 1973.

Robert D Kaplan,Monsoon-The Indian Ocean and Future of American Power, Random House, 2010.

Mote FW. Imperial China, Harvard University Press, 1999.

Muller David G, China as a Maritime Power, Westview Press, Boulder,1983.

Jonathan Green,Murder in The High Himalaya, Public Affairs, 2010.

Nagara Bunn, China's Strategic Culture and Current International Dynamics: Perspective From India, The Rise Of China, Pentagon Press and ORF, 2010.

ShankarKalyani,Nixon, Indira and India: Politics and Beyond, Macmillan Publishers, Delhi,2010.

Nodskov Kim,The Long March to Power, Royal Danish Defence College Publishing House, 2009.

WeiLim Tai,Oil in China: From Self Reliance to Internationalisation,: World Scientific, New Jersey,2010.

Ong Russell, China's Security Interests in the Post-Cold War Era, Curzon Press, London, 2002.

Padfield Peter,The Great Naval Race: Anglo-German Naval Rivalry 1900-1914, Birlinn Limited, Edinburgh, 1974.

Pehrson Christopher J, String of Pearls: Meeting the Challenge of China's Rising Power Across the Asian Littoral, US Army War College, Strategic Studies Institute, 2006.

Lieberman Peter, The Offense-Defense Balance, Interdependence, and War in Power and the Purse: Economic Statecraft, Interdependence and National Security, Jean-Marc F Blanchard, Edward D Mansfield and Norrin M Ripsmaned, Frank Cass Press Portland, 2000.

Politics of China's Environmental Protection: Problems and Progress. Gang Chen. New Jersey: World Scientific, 2009.

Politics of Modern China: Critical Issues in Modern Politics. Zheng Yongnian, Lu Yiyi and WhiteLynn T (ed). London: Routledge, 2010.

Power Realignments in Asia: China India and the United States. Ayres, Alyssa and Mohan C Raja (ed). Los Angeles: Sage Publication, 2009.

Prabhakar W Lawrence S. China's Strategic Culture and Current International Dynamics: Perspective From India, The Rise Of China, Pentagon Press and ORF, 2010.

Prisoner of the State: the Secret Journal of Chinese Premier. ZiyangZhaom, PuBao, Chiang Renee and IgnatiusAdi (ed). New York: Simon and Schuster, 2009.

Question of Balance: Political Context and Military Aspects of the China-Taiwan Dispute. Shlapak David A, Orletsky David T, Reid Toy and Tanner Murray Scot. Pittsburgh: Rand Corporation, 2009.

Recast All Under Heaven, Xiaoyuan Liu, Continuum, New York, 2010.

Regional Inequality in China: Trends Explanations and Policy Responses.

FanShenggen, Kanbur Ravi and ZhangXiaobo (ed). London: Rouledge, 2009.

Rigby Richard Dr. China's Grand Strategy, China's Quest for Global Dominance: Reality or Myth. Ed SandhuMaj Gen PJS. Vij Books, New Delhi.2011.

Rise of China and India in Africa: Challenges Opportunities and Critical Interventions. CheruFantu, Obi Cyril (ed). London: Zed Books, 2010.

Rise of China and Structural Changes in Korea and Asia.Ito Takatoshi Hahn, Chin Hee (ed). Cheltenham: Edward Elgar, 2010.

Rise of China and the Capitalist World Order.Xing Li (ed). Surrey: Ashgate Publishing, 2010.

Rise of China: Responses from Southeast Asia and Japan. Tsunekawa Jun (ed). Tokyo: NIDS, 2009.

Rising China and Security in East Asia :Identity Construction and Security Discourse. Rex Li. London: Routledge, 2009.

Rising China: Opportunity or Strategic Challenge.SandhuMaj Gen (Retd) PJS (ed). New Delhi: USI, 2010.

Role of the European Union in Asia: China and India as Strategic Partners. Gaens Bart, JokelaJuha and LimnellEija (ed). Surrey: Ashgate Publishing Company, 2009.

RongxingGuo. Territorial disputes and Sea Bed Petroleum Exploration: Some Options for the East China Sea, The Brookings Institute Press, Sep 2010.

RoutledgeHandbook of Asian Security Studies.Ganguly, Sumit, Scobell Andrew and Liow Joseph Chinyong (ed). London: Routledge, 2010.

Sadao Asada, From Mahan to Pearl Harbour: The Imperial Japanese Navy and the United States, Naval Institute Press, Annapolis, 2006.

Schencking Charles J, Making Waves: Politics, Propaganda, and the Emergence of the Imperial Japanese Navy, 1868-1922, Stanford University Press, 2005.

Security Challenges Along The Indian Ocean Littoral, UdayBhaskar, KK Agnihotri, Matrix, 2011.

Security Perception and China-India Relations.Li Li. New Delhi: K W Publishers, 2009.

Security Politics in the Asia Pacific, William T Tow, Cambridge, 2010.

Shambaugh David. Modernizing China's Military, University of California Press, 2002.

Shaughnessy Edward L. China: Empire and Civilization, Oxford University Press, 2000.

Shirk Susan L. China: Fragile Superpower Oxford University Press, New York, 2007.

Social Policy and Poverty in East Asia : the Role of Social Security. Midgley James and Tang Kwong-leung (ed). Oxon :Routledge, 2010.

Socialist China Capitalist China: Social Tension and Political Adaptation UnderEconomic Globalisation. Wu Guoguang and Lansdowne Helen (ed). London: Routledge, 2009.

Soft Power: China's Emerging Strategy in International Politics. Mingjiang Li (ed).Lanham: Lexington Books, 2009.

Southeast Asia and the Rise of Chinese and Indian Naval Power: Between Rising Naval Powers. Bateman Sam and Joshua Ho (ed). London: Routledge, 2010.

Speed Philip Andrews, Liao Xuanli and Dannreuther Roland. The Strategic Implications of China's Energy Needs, Oxford University Press, New York, 2002.

Super Power - The Amazing Race Between China's Hare and India's Tortoise, Penguin, 2010.

Sutter Robert G. Chinese Foreign Relations: Power and Diplomacy Since the Cold War, Rowman and Littlefield, Lanham. 2001.

Swanson Bruce. Eighth Voyage of the Dragon: A History of China's Quest for Sea power. Annapolis: Naval Institute Press, 1982.

Tanner Scot Murray, Dumbaugh Kerry B and Easton Ian M, Distracted Antagonists Wary Partners: China and India Assess Their Security Relations, CNA China Studies, September 2011.

Tellis Ashley J, Dr. China's Grand Strategy, China's Quest for Global Dominance: Reality or Myth. Ed SandhuMaj Gen PJS. Vij Books, New Delhi.2011.

Terrill Ross. The New Chinese Empire.Basic Books. New York. 2003. Ibid. pp. 4-8.

The Great Wall At Sea - China's Navy Enters The Twenty First Century, Bernard D Cole, Naval Institute Press, Annapolis, 2001.

The Empire of Lies, Guy Sorman, Encounter Books, 2010.

The Party, Richard McGregor, Penguin Books, 2010.

The Rise of China - Perspectives From Asia and Europe, Ed VP Malik and Jorg Schultz, Pentagon Press, 2008.

The Rise Of Modern China, Immanuel CY Hsu, Oxford University Press, 2000.

The Story of Tibet, Thomas Laird, Atlantic Books, 2006.

The Tragedy Of Tibet, Man Mohan Sharma,Trishul Publications, 2008.

Tibet - The Lost Frontier, Claude Arpi, Lancer Publications, 2008.

Tibet-The Road Ahead, DawaNorbu, Harper Collins, New Delhi, 1997.

Tibet and Its History, HE Richardson, Oxford University Press, London, 1962.

Tibet India and China-Critical Choices: Uncertain Future, Rajesh Kadian, Vision Books, 1999.

Tibet's Last Stand, Warren W Smith Jr, Pentagon Press, 2010.

Tibetan Connundrum, VP Malhotra, Knowledge World, New Delhi, 2006.

Tien Chen Ya. Chinese Military Theory, Mosaic Press, 1992.

Tiget Trap: America's Secret Spy War with China, David Wise, Houghton Mifflin Harcourt, New York, 2011.

Tritle Mathew C. The Growth of PLAN: Impacts and Implications of Regional Naval Expansion, NGS, California, 2007.

US China Economy and Security: Including AfghanistanPakistan and Central Asia. USChina Economic and Security Review Commission. New Delhi: Manas Publication, 2010.

War and Peace in Modern India: a Strategic History of the Nehru Years. RaghavanSrinath. Ranikhet: Permanent Black, 2010.

When China Ruled The Seas - The Treasure Fleet of The Dragon Throne, Louise Levathes, Oxford University Press, 2001.

When China Rules the World: the Rise of the Middle Kingdom and the End of the Western World.Jacques Martin. London: Allen Lane, 2009.

Yoshihara Toshi and Holmes James, Command of the Sea with Chinese Characteristics. Orbis 49, 2005.

Index

A

B

C

J

Jiangkai-class frigates 20
Jin Dynasty 51
Jin-class SSBN 20

K

Kinmen 54
Kunming 58
Kurile Islands 105

L

Lin Biao 18
Liquified Natural Gas 93
Littoral nations 12
Liu Huaqing 105, 125
Liu Shaoqi 54
Look East policy 75
Lushun 21
Luyang II-class Guided Missile Destroyers 20

M

Major Naval Bases 21
  Guangzhou 21
  Huludao 21
  Lushun 21
  Qingdao 21
  Shanghai 21
  Wenzhou 21
  Xiamen 21
  Yulin 21
  Zhanjiang 21
  Zhou Shan 21
Malacca Dilemma 14
Malacca Strait 76, 103
Manchuria 117
Mao Zedong 16, 53
Marianas Islands 105
Maritime diplomacy 12
Maritime strategy 68
Meiji Restoration of 1868 103
Mike Mullen 38, 44
Military Balance 87

www.ingramcontent.com/pod-product-compliance
Lightning Source LLC
Chambersburg PA
CBHW020538270326
41927CB00006B/632